*The Natural History
of New Mexican Mammals*

The Natural History of New Mexican Mammals

James S. Findley

New Mexico Natural History Series

Library of Congress Cataloging-in-Publication Data

Findley, James S. (James Smith), 1926–
  The natural history of New Mexican mammals.

  (New Mexico natural history series)
  Bibliography: p.
  Includes index.
  1. Mammals—New Mexico. I. Title. II. Series.
QL719.N6F56 1987   599'.09789   86-30834
ISBN 0-8263-0957-7
ISBN 0-8263-0958-5 (pbk.)

Contents

Illustration List

Gray Fox	*Urocyon cinereoargenteus*
Black Bear	*Ursus americanus*
Raccoon	*Procyon lotor*
Ring-tailed Cat	*Bassariscus astutus*
Badger	*Taxidea taxus*
Bobcat	*Lynx rufus*
Collared Peccary	*Tayassu tajacu*
Mule Deer	*Odocoileus hemionus*
Elk	*Cervus elaphus*
Pronghorn	*Antilocapra americana*
Mountain Sheep	*Ovis canadensis*

Preface

Two previous books on the mammals of New Mexico have appeared. The first was written by Vernon Bailey, a well-known biologist with the U.S. Bureau of Biological Survey (later known as the National Fish and Wildlife Laboratory, a division of the U.S. Fish and Wildlife Service), and was published in 1932 as number 53 in the series known as North American Fauna. Bailey's work was based on personal experience as well as that of a number of workers from the Bureau, and of other earlier investigators. The 1975 *Mammals of New Mexico*, by myself, A. H. Harris, D. E. Wilson, and C. Jones, was based on all of the earlier studies and collections, as well as on intensive statewide surveys conducted from 1955 until about 1970 with the support of the National Science Foundation and the University of New Mexico. The 1975 work is a technical treatise, intended chiefly for professionals and advanced students. The volume quickly went out of print, and the need for a successor has long been evident. The present work is, in part, a response to that need. Here, I have focused on the natural history of the species that occur in our state. Technical keys for the use of professionals are included, but the orientation of the text is toward outdoors people who want to know about the animals they see. Citations to the primary literature are not included in the text; but comments on secondary sources, which may be found at the end of the book, are included for the benefit of those who would like to read more about our mammals.

Surveys such as this one are made possible by the work of generations of naturalists. Many have been my associates at the University of New Mexico, or colleagues in the American Society of Mammalogists. Bruce Morrison of the New Mexico Department of Game and Fish provided fresh information on the status of exotic mammals in the state. To the extent that the book has merit, a great deal of it must be attributed to the outstanding photography of Larry Brock, Scott Altenbach, and Nina Leen. David Hafner read the entire manuscript and made numerous suggestions for improvement. Donald Duszynski, chairman of the Department of Biology at the University of New Mexico, provided a supportive atmosphere in which the pursuit of scholarly activities was a pleasure. Terry Yates, curator of Mammals at the Museum of Southwestern Biology, has been a spirited friend and colleague who enhanced the pleasures of being a mammalogist in New Mexico. And Tommie Findley, herself an accomplished naturalist, maintained the comfort and tranquillity of our sanctuary in Corrales, where I wrote this book.

Corrales, New Mexico
January 1986

What Are Mammals?

To most people, mammals are warm, furry animals. Sometimes we refer to mammals as "animals," in contrast to birds, fish, and so forth. However, the word *animal* properly refers to all living things that are not plants. The chief distinguishing features of mammals include hair and mammary glands, or breasts, which produce milk for the nourishment of the young. All mammals have hair; even the seemingly hairless whales have a few specialized bristles. Hair provides an insulating layer that prevents heat from readily entering or leaving the mammal's body. Some kinds of mammals have less need for insulation than others, and consequently they have less hair than species that live in cold regions, such as the fur-bearing mammals of the north. All mammals produce milk for the benefit of their young, but the form of the mammary glands may vary considerably. The duck-billed platypus, that strange primitive mammal of Australia, has a series of depressions on the ventral surface into which milk oozes to be lapped up by the babies. Many rodents and other small mammals capable of having large families are provided with eight to ten nipples in rows, and some mammals that have fewer young, such as sheep, bats, and humans, have only two nipples. But all modern species of mammals have both hair and mammary glands.

There are other features that zoologists use to characterize mammals. For example, the teeth of mammals are very distinctive compared to those of other vertebrate animals, such as reptiles, fish, and amphibians. (Birds, of course, have no true teeth.) Mammals usually have teeth of several different shapes that are used for different purposes. For example, a fox or wolf has small nipping teeth in the front of its jaw (the incisors); large stabbing teeth for grasping and subduing prey (the canines); bladelike teeth for slicing meet (the premolars); and broad, grinding teeth (the molars). Other mammals may have some or all of these kinds of teeth, depending upon the way of life of the particular species, and the number and kind of teeth is used as a basis of classification. A few kinds of mammals, such as anteaters, have no teeth at all; a few others, such as some toothed whales and armadillos, have a mouthful of teeth which are all of the same kind. Teeth are made of very hard material and are easily fossilized. As a result, much of our knowledge of the fossil history of mammals is based upon their teeth.

Mammalogists use a shortened notation for describing the kinds and numbers of mammalian teeth. For example, the dentition of a coyote is described by the following: 3/3, 1/1, 4/4, 2/3. This means that the animal has 3 upper and 3 lower incisors, 1 upper and 1 lower canine, 4 upper and 4 lower premolars, and 2 upper and 3 lower molars on one side of the mouth.

When we say that mammals are "warm-blooded" we mean that their bodies are noticeably warm, often warmer than the air temperature, and that they remain warm most of the time, in contrast to animals such as snakes, lizards, frogs, and fish, which cool down if the air or water cools down. Animals, like mammals, that have a more or less constant temperature are referred to homeotherms. However, most so-called homeotherms don't really have a constant temperature. The normal temperature of a human, for example, is said to be 98.6° F; but, in fact, that varies a degree or two, even in a healthy individual. And some mammals have tremendous fluctuations in their temperatures, such as the ground squirrels and bats that go into hibernation in the winter and allow their bodies to drop within a few degrees of freezing. Nonetheless, when necessary, these species can voluntarily bring their temperatures back up to operating level by generating heat within their bodies by muscular contraction and by biochemical means. Animals that can do this are referred to as endotherms: creatures which can produce their own heat internally without the aid of the outside environment. It is probably most correct to call mammals endotherms. Birds are the only other animals that are all capable endotherms, although a few species of fish, such as tuna and mackerel, may have limited abilities along this line, as may a few moths.

Most mammals are live-bearers: the females bear young mammals, not eggs. There is one exception: the platypus and its relative, the spiny anteater, which live in Australia and New Guinea, lay eggs, much like those of reptiles. All other mammals produce tiny shell-less eggs which, after they are fertilized by a sperm, lodge in the uterus of the female and develop into a small individual before being born. While in the uterus, the baby derives most of its nourishment from the circulatory system of the mother. Some mammals are born in a very immature state of development, being naked, blind, deaf, and unable to walk or otherwise take care of themselves. Such animals are spoken of as being *altricial*. Examples are many rodents, bats, and shrews. Other kinds of mammals are born in a much more advanced state of development, with full coats of hair and with vision, hearing, and locomotor ability. Such species are referred to as being *precocial*. Examples are deer, cattle, horses, jackrabbits, and some kinds of rodents, such as guinea pigs and porcupines. Mammals may produce from one to fifteen babies per litter. The number depends upon a variety of factors including the risk of predation and the amount of care that the adults give the young. Those species that produce few young tend to suffer less predation, and their young are cared for by the parent or parents for a relatively long time. Species which produce large numbers of babies per litter are often those kinds that have high mortality from predators, and whose young leave the natal shelter at an early age. However, regardless of the reproductive strategy followed by a given species, all successful kinds manage to replace themselves on a one-for-one basis over the long haul.

The average mammal is probably about the size of a pack rat, but the size range among mammals is tremendous. The smallest known mammal is probably a species of shrew which weighs about 2 grams. The largest mammal, and probably the largest animal of any sort that has ever lived, is the blue whale, which may weigh up to 112 tons: over 112 *million* grams, or 56 million times heavier than the shrew! No other group of animals has such extreme differences between the largest and smallest members. Large size is advantageous for endothermic animals because the larger the animal the less surface area it has per unit of volume, and there is relatively less surface from which heat can be lost. Therefore, larger animals are more efficient endotherms. Also, large animals have fewer predators and need less food per unit of weight. But there must be some advantages to being small or there wouldn't be so many small mammals, such as mice, rats, shrews, tiny bats, and so on. Small mammals produce more young more frequently, and they may be able to adapt through evolutionary change more rapidly than large ones. Also, small mammals may be able to responds to periods of abundant resources more rapidly than large ones, through rapid population growth.

Mammals are found in almost all parts of the world. Exceptions are the continent of Antarctica and some remote oceanic islands where the only mammals may be humans and some of their commensals, such as rats or mice, and domestic mammals, such as cats, goats, and the like. Various species of whales are found in all seas. The range of habitats occupied by mammals is also great, and some are found at practically all elevations, and in extremes of heat and cold. Ability to tolerate a wide variety of environmental circumstances, because of sophisticated temperature regulation and water conservation, is probably one of the keys to the present success of mammals as a class.

A recent tabulation reveals that there are 4,206 species of mammals living on Earth today. Of these, a huge number, 42 percent, are rodents. Next in abundance are bats, 22 percent. Of somewhat lesser number are insectivores, carnivores, and hooved mammals. Number of kinds, however, is not the only measure of importance of a group. In number of individuals, rodents and bats are probably also in the lead. When weight, or biomass, is taken into account some other groups may come to the fore in certain areas. Hooved grazing mammals probably outweigh rodents in some of the world's grasslands, although exact measures are not easy to come by.

Spotted Bat
Euderma maculatum
(Nina Leen)

Brazilian Free-tailed Bat
Tadarida brasiliensis
(J. Scott Altenbach)

Pallid Bat
Antrozous pallidus
(J. Scott Altenbach)

Hoary Bat
Lasiurus cinereus
(J. Scott Altenbach)

Desert Cottontail
Sylvilagus auduboni
(Larry Brock)

Red Squirrel
Tamiasciurus hudsonicus
(Larry Brock)

Least Chipmunk
Eutamias minimus
(James S. Findley)

Black-tailed Prairie Dog
Cynomys ludovicianus
(Larry Brock)

Mantled Ground Squirrel
Spermophilus lateralis
(Larry Brock)

White-tailed Antelope Ground Squirrel
Ammospermophilus leucurus
(David J. Hafner)

Spotted Ground Squirrel
Spermophilus spilosoma
(Larry Brock)

Botta Pocket Gopher
Thomomys bottae
(Larry Brock)

Ord Kangaroo Rat
Dipodomys ordii
(James S. Findley)

Piñon Mouse
Peromyscus truei
(James S. Findley)

Silky Pocket Mouse
Perognathus flavus
(James S. Findley)

Northern Grasshopper Mouse
Onychomys leucogaster
(James S. Findley)

White-throated Wood Rat
Neotoma albigula
(James S. Findley)

Western Jumping Mouse
Zapus princeps
(James S. Findley)

Porcupine
Erethizon dorsatum
(Larry Brock)

Coyote
Canis latrans
(Larry Brock)

Red Fox
Vulpes vulpes
(Larry Brock)

Kit Fox
Vulpes macrotis
(Larry Brock)

Gray Fox
Urocyon cinereoargenteus
(Larry Brock)

Black Bear
Ursus americanus
(Larry Brock)

Raccoon
Procyon lotor
(Larry Brock)

Ring-tailed Cat
Bassariscus astutus
(James S. Findley)

Badger
Taxidea taxus
(Larry Brock)

Bobcat
Lynx rufus
(Larry Brock)

Collared Peccary
Tayassu tajacu
(Larry Brock)

Mule Deer
Odocoileus hemionus
(Larry Brock)

Elk
Cervus elaphus
(Larry Brock)

Pronghorn
Antilocapra americana
(Larry Brock)

Mountain Sheep
Ovis canadensis
(Larry Brock)

Mammals in New Mexico

One hundred forty-nine species of native mammals, not counting humans, occur in New Mexico, or have in the recent past. An additional five to seven kinds live here as a result of intentional or accidental introduction by humans. And, of course, domestic livestock, especially cattle and sheep, have a huge ecological impact on most of the state.

About 4 percent of the known kinds of land mammals occur in New Mexico, but since only about 0.3 percent (three-tenths of 1 percent) of Earth's inhabited land lies within our borders, it is clear that our mammalian fauna is very rich indeed, over ten times richer than it would be if mammalian species were distributed at random over Earth's land surface. Few other places of comparable size in the world support as many different kinds of mammals. Why should this be?

The answer has to do with the topography of New Mexico, and also with its history. Elevational extremes in the state range from less than four thousand feet above sea level in the lower Pecos Valley to over thirteen thousand feet in the high Sangre de Cristo Mountains. Such a gradient has a profound effect upon local climates. Air at higher elevations is less dense and is cooler, so that mountains are cooler throughout the year than lowlands. Also, mountains interpose barriers to the flow of air that crosses the state. When air currents from the southwest encounter a mountain range, the air rises and cools; and since cool air has less capacity to hold moisture than warm air, rain falls at the higher elevations, which are thus better watered. When the air descends on the other side of the mountain it warms, and as it does so it takes up water from the land. The leeward sides of mountains thus tend to be rainshadows that are drier than they would be if the mountain wasn't there. Thus, topographic relief causes zonation in temperature and rainfall, and these changes result in the existence of different communities of plants at different elevations and on different sides of mountains. This vegetational diversity is reflected in the animal life as well, since ultimately the animals are dependent on the plants for survival.

Historical changes in climate and landscape have played their part in enhancing mammalian diversity in New Mexico as well. In the late phases of the Glacial Age (the Pleistocene Epoch), which ended approximately ten thousand years ago, climates were much cooler and more moist, and forested zones descended to much lower elevations in the Southwest. Pine and mixed coniferous forest, and perhaps spruce and fir in some places, occurred over the lower elevations so that the now isolated montane forests were one interconnected. Under those circumstances, northern forest-loving species of mammals were able to penetrate to southern parts of the state, and forest-inhabiting southern species from the Mexican Plateau were able to move freely to more northern areas. As the climate progressively warmed and forested habitats retreated to the higher elevations, those species became trapped, or isolated, on various mountains that were large enough to provide a refuge of suitable habitat. When forested habitats were widespread, grassland and desert species were much more limited in their distribution in the state than they are today; and they occupied refuges in the Great Plains, the Sonoran and Chihuahuan deserts, and perhaps in the Great Basin. With the return of warmer and more arid conditions, those lowland species moved back into the state from their separate refuges, greatly enriching the fauna of grassland- and desert-adapted species. Undoubtedly, this process has been repeated a number of times, with each such cycle perhaps adding to biological diversity.

Major Habitats in New Mexico

Habitat types in the state have been variously categorized. One of the early attempts to classify biological regions in the Southwest was that of the famous nineteenth-century American naturalist Clinton Hart Merriam, whose life-zone system was widely used for many years. The realization that the Merriam life zones were based on faulty information, and were oversimplifications of a very complex situation, has led to their abandonment by most biologists. But there is no doubt that elevational changes in vegetation in our region are very pronounced and can be described in a general way by the recognition of a relatively few life-zone categories. For the purpose of describing mammalian habitats in this book I have used seven terms. These are *alpine zone, spruce-fir forest, mixed coniferous forest, ponderosa forest, woodland, grassland,* and *desert.*

The alpine zone is a treeless community of grasses, sedges, perennial forbs, and dwarfed shrubs, which occurs at the highest elevations in the Sangre de Cristo Mountains. This habitat is very limited in area in New Mexico, but is much more widespread in Colorado. Limited treeless areas, or "balds," occur on a few other mountains, such as the Magdalenas and Sierra Blanca; and these may be alpine meadows left over from the Pleistocene that have not yet been reinvaded by forest, but they are not above climatic tree line.

Spruce-fir forest is comprised chiefly of Alpine or corkbark fir (*Abies lasiocarpa*) and Englemann spruce (*Picea englemanni*). It covers the higher elevations of Mount Taylor and the San Juan, Jemez, Sangre de Cristo,

7

and Sandía mountains, as well as the higher southern ranges such as the Sacramentos, Mogollons, and White mountains. Small stands may occur on the coolest and highest parts of smaller ranges.

Mixed coniferous forest is characterized by white fir (*Abies concolor*), Douglas-fir (*Pseudotsuga menziesii*), ponderosa pine (*Pinus ponderosa*), and Rocky Mountain juniper (*Juniperus scopulorum*). It is widespread below the spruce-fir forest on most of the larger mountain ranges.

Ponderosa forest is comprised mostly of pure stands of ponderosa pine. Sheltered canyons in this zone may support small stands of Douglas-fir. Ponderosa forests are generally open and have a relatively good ground cover of grasses. These forests occur below the mixed coniferous communities.

Woodland is one of the most widespread communities in our state above the grasslands. It is comprised chiefly of one-seeded juniper (*Juniperus monosperma*) and piñon pine (*Pinus edulis*). In more southern areas, various species of live oak (*Quercus* spp.) may join these two small coniferous trees.

Grassland covers most of New Mexico. To an easterner, or a person from the central grasslands of Kansas or Nebraska, the characterization of what we have designated here as grassland may seem like stretching the definition. However, there are many species of grasses in the state, and over vast areas they are the dominant form of vegetation and set the living conditions for the animal life. Many of New Mexico's grasslands, especially those at lower elevations, have been severely degraded by domestic livestock since the late 1600s, and it seems unlikely that some of these severely abused places will ever recover their original appearance. In lower and warmer places where the grasses have been destroyed by overgrazing, soil erosion has removed the basis of recovery, and creosote bush (*Larrea divaricata*), a characteristic plant of southwestern deserts, has replaced the grass, probably permanently so far as humans are concerned. This kind of change has made some former grassland areas appear to be desert. Nonetheless, no matter what the newly arrived New Yorker may call it, there is no true desert around Albuquerque, only grassland.

In the Southwest, desert is defined as those places where water is so limited that grasses are scarce, and various species of widely spaced shrubs take over. Southwestern deserts are characterized by the presence of creosote bush, which grows over vast lowland and foothill areas in the southern part of New Mexico. The desert in New Mexico is considered part of the Chihuahuan Desert, which extends southward over the central part of the Mexican Plateau and also into the trans-Pecos region of Texas. Soapweed (*Yucca elata*), the state flower, is characteristic of this desert, as are a variety of acacias, mesquites, and agaves or century plants. A great deal of the area covered by creosote is actually degraded grassland, and true Chihuahuan desert is probably limited to relatively small parts of the lower Rio Grande and Pecos valleys.

Within each of the zones described, there are special communities that are dependent upon the presence of bodies of water such as streams and rivers. In the spruce-fir zone, these riparian communities are usually made up of willows (*Salix*), alders (*Alnus*) and blue spruces (*Picea pungens*). In somewhat lower zones, these trees are joined by narrow-leaved cottonwood (*Populus angustifolia*) and box elder (*Acer negundo*). Beginning in the woodland zone, and extending along watercourses into the grasslands, the dominant tree is the valley cottonwood (*Populus wislizenii*), which forms extensive gallery forests, especially in the middle Rio Grande Valley. At still more southern sites, valley cottonwood may be joined by sycamore (*Platanus wrightii*), walnut (*Juglans microcarpa*), and ash (*Fraxinus velutina*).

Identifying Mammals

Mammals are much more difficult to identify than birds, reptiles, amphibians, or plants. Partly, this is so because most mammals are very secretive and nocturnal, and the average person, even someone who spends a good deal of time outdoors, sees relatively few of them. Most mammals do not give you the opportunity to study them with binoculars while you consult a field manual, and it is rare to get your hands on one so that you can examine it at leisure. Even if you do have the opportunity to examine a small mammal closely, you may find that the identifying features are the teeth, or the cranial anatomy, which you cannot see without dissection and magnification. Added to this difficulty is the complication caused by the existence of numerous similar and closely related species that even professional mammalogists have trouble in identifying. For example, in New Mexico there are nine species of deer mice of the genus *Peromyscus* which are very much like one another, often distinguishable only by slight differences in the proportions of ears or tails. Many of the larger mammals, however—the ones you are likely to see while hiking through the countryside—are more readily identified.

A device used by biologists to identify organisms is called a key. Such a key is a written outline of all the animals to be identified, arranged as a series of contrasting statements about how the animal may appear. Each pair of statements requires one to make a choice between, for example, "color black, or color white." If the animal in question is black, one is told to go to step B; if it is white, to step C.

Eventually, you make a choice which leads you to the correct name of the animal. The following key to New Mexican mammals is one of these devices. It is a technical key because it requires you to have a specimen of the mammal to examine; it may require you to look at cranial characteristics; and it requires the use of a technical vocabulary. The glossary at the end of the book will help with the terminology. If you are not able to pursue this key, you can probably learn the identity of the animal by taking it to an expert at one of the state's colleges or universities, or to a biologist at the New Mexico Department of Game and Fish. The educational institutions which today are best able to help with these identifications are the University of New Mexico in Albuquerque, New Mexico State University in Las Cruces, Western New Mexico University in Silver City, and Eastern New Mexico University in Portales. You may also wish to contact the New Mexico Museum of Natural History.

Key to the Identification of New Mexican Mammals

Key to Orders

1. Forelimbs modified as wings, canines large and prominent, great-
    est skull length less than 35 mm: . . . . .Order Chiroptera (Bats).
    Forelimbs not modified as wings; if canines large and prominent,
    then greatest skull length greater than 35 mm: 2
2. Back covered with bony plates; teeth a row of small, similar pegs:
    . . . . .Order Edentata, *Dasypus novemcinctus* (Armadillo).
    Back not covered with bony plates, teeth not as above: 3
3. No upper incisors or, if present, teeth bunodont and skull large;
    feet protected by at least two hooves per foot: . . . .
    .Order Artiodactyla (Hooved mammals).
    Upper incisors present; if hooves present, then only one per foot:
   4
4. Incisors 1/1: . . . . .Order Rodentia (Rodents).
    Incisors more than 1/1:. 5
5. Incisors 2/1; tail length less than ear length:. . . . .
    . . . . .Order Lagomorpha (Rabbits, hares, pikas).
    Incisors more than 2/1; if tail length less than ear length (as in
    bears), then large prominent canines present: 6
6. Upper and lower incisors procumbent, hooklike, and with second-
    ary cusps (when unworn); eyes minute; snout long and pointed
    and extending well in front of mouth; total length less than 200
    mm: . . . . .Order Insectivora, family Soricidae (Shrews).

Upper and lower incisors not as described as above; eyes "normal" size; snout not long and pointed, not extending far in front of mouth; total length more than 200 mm: 7

7. Incisors 5/4; tail long, naked, and scaly; ears large and naked: . . . . .Order Marsupialia, *Didelphis virginiana* (Opossum).

    Incisors less than 5/4; tail and ears not as above: 8

8. Canines large and extending well beyond level of other teeth; pentadactyl feet provided with claws:. . . . .

    . . . . .Order Carnivora (Carnivores).

    Canines, if present, small and not extending beyond level of other teeth; a single hoof-covered toe on each foot: . . . .

    . . . . .Order Perissodactyla, genus *Equus* (Horses).

Key to Shrews of New Mexico

1. Total teeth, twenty-eight; three unicuspids in each maxillary tooth-row:. . . . .*Notiosorex crawfordi.*

    Total teeth, thirty; four unicuspids in each maxillary tooth-row:. . .

    . . . .*Cryptotis parva.*

    Total teeth, thirty-two; five unicuspids in each maxillary tooth-row:

    . . . .*(Sorex)*, 2

2. Third and forth unicuspids approximately equal in size:. 3

    Third unicuspid obviously smaller than the fourth: 4

3. Each upper unicuspid tooth provided with a pigmented ridge running from apex of tooth lingually to the medial cingulum of tooth, and there ending in a small pigmented cusplet; unicuspids uncrowded, broad, and not very high-crowned; underparts brownish or buffy (not whitish):. . . . .*Sorex cinereus.*

    Each upper unicuspid without lingually directed pigmented ridge or medial cusplet; unicuspids crowded, narrow (from front to back), appearing high-crowned; underparts whitish:. 6

4. Condylobasal length 20 mm or more; hindfoot fringed with stiff hairs; blackish above, white below:. . . . .*Sorex palustris.*

    Condylobasal length 18 mm or less; hindfoot without fringe of stiff hairs; grayish or brownish above, tan or gray below: 5

5. Condylobasal length less than 15 mm; total length usually less than 100 mm; hindfoot 11 mm or less:. . . . .*Sorex nanus.*

    Condylobasal length more than 15 mm; total length more than 100 mm; hindfoot 12 mm or more: . . . .*Sorex monticolus.*

6. Each upper front incisor with a small medial tine:. .*Sorex arizonae.*

    Upper incisor without medial tines:. . . . .*Sorex merriami.*

Key to Bats of New Mexico

1. Nose leaf present; tail vertebrae not extending to edge of interfemoral membrane; no diastema in upper incisor series, bony
plate complete in front: . . . . .Family Phyllostomatidae, 2
No nose leaf; tail extending at least to edge of interfemoral membrane; diastema in upper incisor row present; if absent, then tail
extending well posterior to edge of interfemoral membrane: . . .3

2. Tail extremely reduced; zygomatic arch complete; two lower incisors on each side:. . . . .*Leptonycteris sanborni.*
Tail more than 10 mm: zygomatic arch incomplete; no lower in-
cisors: . . . .*Choeronycteris mexicana.*

3. Tail extending conspicuously beyond free edge of interfemoral
membrane: . . . . .Family Molossidae, 4
Tail extending at most a few mm beyond free edge of interfemoral
membrane:. . . . . .Family Vespertilionidae, 7

4. Forearm more than 65 mm; upper lips without deep vertical
grooves; palate without anterior emargination:. .*Eumops perotis.*
Forearm less than 65 mm; upper lips with deep vertical grooves;
palate with anterior emargination: 5

5. Forearm less than 45 mm; ears not united at base; second phalanx
of fourth finger more than 5 mm; breadth of rostrum markedly
greater than interorbital breadth: . . . .*Tadarida brasiliensis.*
Forearm greater than 45 mm; ears united at base; second phalanx
of fourth finger less than 5 mm; breadth of rostrum little more
than interorbital breadth:. 6

6. Skull longer than 21 mm:. . . . .*Nyctinomops macrotis.*
Skull less than 21 mm: . . . .*Nyctinomops femorosacca.*

7. One upper incisor on each side: 8
Two upper incisors on each side:. 11

8. Total teeth, twenty-eight; ears long and naked; upper surface of
interfemoral membrane largely naked: . . . . . .*Antrozous pallidus.*
Total teeth, thirty to thirty-two; ears short, rounded, and partly
furred; upper surface of interfemoral membrane wholly or at
least one-half furred:. 9

9. One pair of upper premolars:. . . . .*Lasiurus ega.*
Two pairs of upper premolars (first of which is minute, medially
displaced, and not visible in lateral view of tooth-row): 10

10. Skull longer than 15 mm: . . . .*Lasiurus cinereus.*
Skull shorter than 15 mm: . . . .*Lasiurus borealis.*

11. Interfemoral membrane densely furred dorsally for more than one-half its length; fur black, tipped with white: ....*Lasionycteris noctivagans.* Interfemoral membrane furred for, at most, its basal one-third; fur not black tipped with white:.............................12

12. Cheek teeth (postcanine teeth) 6/6: ....(*Myotis*), 17 Cheek teeth fewer than 6/6: 13

13. Length of ear more than 25 mm:...........................14 Length of ear less than 25 mm: 16

14. Dorsal color black with three large white spots; postcanine teeth 5–5: ....*Euderma maculatum.* Dorsal color not as above; postcanine teeth 5/6: 15

15. A pair of anterior accessory lappets between base of ears:....... ....*Idionycteris phyllotis.* No anterior accessory lappets between bases of ears:........... ....*Plecotis townsendii.*

16. One pair of upper premolars:...................*Eptesicus fuscus.* Two pairs of upper premolars: ....*Pipistrellus hesperus.*

17. Calcar with well-marked keel: ....18 Calcar without well-marked keel: 20

18. Ventral surface of plagiopatagium furred to elbow:............. ....*Myotis volans.* Ventral surface of plagiopatagium not furred to elbow:........19

19. Rostral breadth less than 5.1 mm; skull length less than 13.5 mm: ....*Myotis californicus.* Rostral breadth more than 5.1 mm; skull length more than 13.5 mm:.............................*Myotis leibii.*

20. Free edge of uropatagium with distinct fringe of macroscopically visible short hairs:.......................*Myotis thysanodes.* Free edge of uropatagium without a distinct fringe of macroscopically visible hairs: 21

21. Well-developed sagittal crest present:.............*Myotis velifer.* No well-developed sagittal crest:..........................22

22. Ears more than 16 mm: ....23 Ears less than 16 mm:.....................................24

23. Ears black: ....*Myotis evotis.* Ears brownish (may be dark, but not black):.....*Myotis auriculus.*

24. Dorsal fur usually with a slight sheen; mastoid breadth usually 7.5 mm or more: ....*Myotis lucifugus.* Dorsal fur usually lacking a sheen; mastoid breadth generally 7.4 mm or less: ....*Myotis yumanensis.*

Key to Lagomorphs of New Mexico

1. Ear pinna as broad as long; no visible tail; premolars 2/2: . . . .
. . . . .Ochotonidae, *Ochotona princeps.*
Ear pinna very long; tail short but obvious; premolars 3/2: . . . . . .
. . . . .Leporidae, 2

2. Interparietal bone fused to parietals in adults; length of hindfoot
usually 130 mm or more:. . . . . .genus *Lepus*, 3
Interparietal bone distinct; hindfoot usually 105 mm or less: . . . .
genus *Sylvilagus,* 6

3. No anterior projection on supraorbital process, or if present, very
small; skull length less than 80 mm; ear less than 75 mm: . . . . .
. . . .*Lepus americanus.*
Prominent anterior projection on supraorbital process; skull length
more than 90 mm; ear more than 100 mm:. 4

4. Whitish ventral color meeting dark dorsal color along a distinct line
well up on flanks; ears without distinct black tip:. . . .*L. callotis.*
Light ventral coloration gradually blending into color of dorsum;
ears with black tip: 5

5. Top of tail with black stripe that extends onto the back: . . . .
. . . .*L. californicus.*
Top of tail without dark dorsal stripe: . . . .*L. townsendii.*

6. Hindfoot usually 92 mm or less; bullar length usually 11.5 mm or
more; hindfoot/ear ratio 1.50 or less; ear/total-length ratio 0.14 or
more; bullar-length/basilar-length ratio 0.22 or more; slides of
interpterygoid fossa concave with slight shelf:. . . . .
. . . .*Sylvilagus auduboni.*
Hindfoot usually 92 or more; bullar length 12.3 mm or less; hind-
foot/ear ratio 1.35 or more; ear/total-length ratio 0.18 or less;
bullar-length/basilar-length ratio 0.23 or less; slides of interpterygoid fossa straight, little or no shelf: 7

7. Supraoccipital shield convex or pointed posteriorly; anterior segment of parietal-squamosal suture straight; basilar length usually 57 mm or less; mean earlength 65 mm or less; mean hind-
foot/ear ratio, 1.48 or more; bullar/basilar-length ratio usually
0.21 or more:. . . . .*Sylvilagus nuttalli.*
Supraoccipital shield truncate or emarginate; anterior segment of
parietal-squamosal suture convoluted; basilar length usually 52
mm or more; mean earlength 65 mm or more; mean hindfoot/ear
ratio, 1.47 or less: . . . .*Sylvilagus floridanus.*

Key to Major Groups of Rodents in New Mexico

1. Infraorbital foramen very large, larger than foramen magnum:. .2
   Infraorbital foramen smaller than foramen magnum:. 3
2. Dorsal hairs in part modified to form stout spines:. . . . .
   . . . . .Erethizontidae, *Erethizon dorsatum.*
   Dorsal hairs not so modified: . . . .Capromyidae, *Myocastor coypus.*
3. Tail dorsoventrally flattened, broad and naked:. . . . .
   . . . . .Castoridae, *Castor canadensis.*
   Tail not dorsoventrally flattened:. 4
4. Infraorbital foramen a vertically elongate V-shaped slit; cheek teeth
   3/3: . . . . .Superfamily Muroidea.
   Infraorbital foramen not as above; cheek teeth more than 3/3: . .5
5. Infraorbital foramen an ovoid hole; hind feet elongate; tail elongate, naked, and scaly: . . . . .Family Zapodidae, *Zapus.*
   Infraorbital foramen a very small canal or round hole; tail, if elongate, not naked and scaly:. 6
6. External fur-lined cheek pouches present; prominent postorbital
   processes lacking: 7
   External fur-lined cheek pouches absent; prominent preorbital processes present: . . . . .Family Sciuridae.
7. Skull heavy, zygomatic breadth greater than mastoid breadth; tail
   less than three-quarters head and body length; claws on forefeet
   at least somewhat enlarged for digging:. . . .Family Geomyidae.
   Skull light; zygomatic breadth less than mastoid breadth; tail more
   than three-quarters head and body length; claws on forefeet not
   greatly modified for digging: . . . . .Family Heteromyidae.

Key to Squirrels of New Mexico

1. Tail less than one-third total length, condylobasal length more than
   60 mm:. 2
   Tail more than one-half total length; condylobasal length less than
   60 mm:. 4
2. Maxillary tooth-rows approximately parallel; condylobasal length
   more than 80 mm; front feet with four clawed digits: . . . .
   . . . .*Marmota flaviventris.*
   Maxillary tooth-rows converging posteriorly; condylobasal length
   less than 70 mm; front feet with five clawed digits: . . . .
   . . . .*Cynomys,* 3

3. Tip of tail black:. . . . .*Cynomys ludovicianus.*
   Tip of tail white or light gray: . . . .*Cynomys gunnisoni.*
4. Zygomatic arches nearly parallel to one another: 5
   Zygomatic arches convergent anteriorly:. .8
5. Total length usually less than 360 mm; P3 vestigial or absent:. . . .
   . . . .*Tamiasciurus hudsonicus.*
   Total length usually more than 450 mm; P3 usually well developed:
  6
6. Venter orangish, reddish, or buffy: . . . .*Sciurus niger.*
   Venter white or black:. 7
7. Ears with prominent tufts of hair on ends; usually five cheek teeth
   in upper tooth-row: . . . .*Sciurus aberti.*
   Ears without tufts; usually four cheek teeth in upper tooth-row:
   . . . .*Sciurus arizonensis.*
8. Sides of head striped; posterior border of zygomatic process of
   maxillary opposite P3: . . . .*Eutamias,* 9
   Sides of head not striped; posterior border of zygomatic process of
   maxillary opposite M1:. 13
9. Dorsal stripes obscure, not clearly delineated:. . .*Eutamias dorsalis.*
   Dorsal stripes clearly marked:. 10
10. Condylobasal length less than 30.5 mm; hindfoot usually 32 mm or
    less; upper lip buffy: . . . .*Eutamias minimus.*
    Condylobasal length more than 31 mm; hindfoot usually 33 mm or
    more; upper lip whitish: 11
11. Hind feet grayish dorsally; in Gallinas, Capitan, Sacramento, and
    Guadalupe mountains:. . . . .*Eutamias canipes.*
    Hind feet buffy dorsally; not distributed as above:. 12
12. Neck with grayish dorsal wash; south of U.S. 66 and west of Rio
    Grande:. . . . .*Eutamias cinereicollis.*
    Neck without grayish wash; not distributed as above:. . . . .
    . . . .*Eutamias quadrivittatus.*
13. Dorsal pattern incorporating some continuous stripes: 14
    Dorsal pattern spotted or mottled: 18
14. Dorsal pattern of stripes and rows of spots:. . . . .
    . . . .*Spermophilus tridecemlineatus.*
    Dorsal pattern of two white stripes; not spots: 15
15. Tail brownish ventrally, longer than 85 mm:. . . . .
    . . . .*Spermophilus lateralis.*
    Tail whitish, grayish, or blackish ventrally, less than 85 mm:. . .16
16. Tail dark below:. . . . .*Ammospermophilus harrisii.*
    Tail whitish below: 17

17. East of Rio Grande: . . . .*Ammospermophilus interpres.*
    West of Rio Grande:. . . . .*Ammospermophilus leucurus.*
18. Tail long and bushy, more than 135 mm; mottled grayish dorsally:
    . . . .*Spermophilus variegatus.*
    Tail shorter-haired, less than 135 mm; spotted dorsally: 19
19. Spots arranged in many rows: . . . .*Spermophilus mexicanus.*
    Spots irregularly arranged: . . . .*Spermophilus spilosoma.*

Key to Pocket Gophers of New Mexico

1. Upper incisors lacking conspicuous longitudinal grooves: . . . .
   . . . .*Thomomys,* 2
   Upper incisors with one or more conspicuous longitudinal grooves:
  4
2. Found in the higher parts of the Animas Mountains, Hidalgo
   County: . . . .*Thomomys umbrinus.*
   Not found in the higher Animas: 3
3. Color yellowish, brownish, or blackish; anterior openings of infra-
   orbital canals not posterior to anterior palatine foramina:. . . . . .
   . . . .*Thomomys bottae.*
   Color grayish or brownish; anterior openings of infraorbital canals
   posterior to anterior palatine foramina:. . . . .*Thomomys talpoides.*
4. Upper incisors each with one longitudinal groove:. . . . .
   . . . .*Pappogeomys castanops.*
   Upper incisors each with two longitudinal grooves:. . . . .
   . . . .*Geomys bursarius.*

Key to Pocket Mice and Rats of New Mexico

1. Soles of hind feet densely haired; interparietal less than ¼ greatest
   width of skull; maxilla with enlarged and laterally projecting
   flange above root of zygomatic arch:. . . . . . .genus *Dipodomys,* 2
   Soles of hind feet naked, or furred only to plantar surface; interparietal more than ¼ greatest width of skull; maxilla with very
   small laterally projecting flange: 4
2. Maxillary breadth more than 22 mm; tip of tail white:. . . . .
   . . . .*Dipodomys spectabilis.*
   Maxillary breadth less than 22 mm; tip of tail not white: 3
3. Hindfoot with four toes; lateral aspect of dentary ramus molded so
   as to suggest the bases of the teeth:. . . . . . .*Dipodomys merriami.*

Hindfoot with five toes; lateral aspect of dentary ramus flatter:
. . . .*Dipodomys ordii.*
4. Bullae larger, in dorsal view comprising more than one-half of
transverse distance across skull through middle of interparietal;
hair on end of tail usually not longer than hair near base of tail:
. . . . .genus *Perognathus,* 5
Bullae smaller, in dorsal view less than half of transverse distance
across skull through middle of interparietal; hairs on end of tail
longer than those at base or not: . . . . .genus *Chaetodipus,* 6
5. Length of tail usually 60 mm or more; total length usually 120 mm
or more; length of skull usually more than 21 mm: . . . .
. . . .*Perognathus flavescens.*
Length of tail usually less than 60 mm; total length usually less
than 120 mm; length of skull usually less than 21 mm: . . . .
. . . .*Perognathus flavus.*
6. Hairs at end of tail not longer than those near base; tubes of audi-
tory bullae projecting lateral of mastoids in dorsal view: . . . . . .
. . . .*Chaetodipus hispidus.*
Hairs at end of tail noticeably longer than those near base; tubes of
auditory bullae not projecting as above: .7
7. Rump spines usually present; rocky habitats: 8
Rump spines absent; habitat various: 9
8. Total length more than 180 mm; premaxilla extending distinctly
farther posteriorly than nasal: . . . .*Chaetodipus nelsoni.*
Total length less than 180 mm; premaxilla extending posteriorly
about the same disance as nasal: . . . .*Chaetodipus intermedius.*
9. Tail much longer than head and body; head and body usually more
than 95 mm; interparietal width equal to or less than least inter-
orbital width: . . . .*Chaetodipus baileyi.*
Tail slightly longer than head and body; head and body usually
less than 95 mm; interparietal width exceeds least interorbital
width: . . . .*Chaetodipus penicillatus.*

Key to Muroid Rodents of New Mexico

1. Cusps of upper molars in three longitudinally arranged rows: . . .
. . . . .Family Muridae, 2
Cusps of upper molars in two longitudinally arranged rows: . . .4
2. Length of skull less than 20 mm: . . . .*Mus musculus.*
Length of skull more than 20 mm: . . . .*Rattus,* 3

3. Temporal ridges more or less straight and parallel to one another as they cross the parietal bone; tail length usually less than length of head and body: ....*Rattus norvegicus.*
Temporal ridges bowed laterally and diverging posteriorly as they cross the parietal bone; tail length as long as or longer than length of head and body:......................*Rattus rattus.*

4. Occlusal surface of each molar with a complicated pattern of triangular and other shaped figures outlined in enamel enclosing dentine lakes; occlusal surface flat: 5
Occlusal surface of each molar with a series of bunodont cusps, which may disappear with wear, leaving a few relatively formless dentine lakes bordered with enamel; occlusal surface usually not flat:.....................Family Cricetidae (part), 18

5. Dorsal border of infraorbital forming a posteriorly directed notch when viewed from above; incisive foramina longer than occlusal surface of molars and about as wide as distance between molar rows:............................Family Cricetidae (part), 6
Dorsal border of infraorbital foramen not as above; incisive foramina shorter than occlusal surface of molars, narrower than distance between molar rows:.............Family Arvicolidae, 11

6. Molars with V-shaped rëentrant angles; without conspicuous temporal ridges on parietal bones; ears prominent and naked; color pattern sharply bicolored:........................*Neotoma*, 7
Molars without V-shaped rëentrant angles; with conspicuous temporal ridges on parietal bones; ears partly hidden in fur and haired; color not sharply bicolored: ....*Sigmodon*, 31

7. Tail conspicuously bushy: ....*Neotoma cinerea.*
Tail not conspicuously bushy:...............................8

8. Dorsal color steel gray in adults; nasal septum (plate extending dorsally between palatine foramina) intact:...*Neotoma micropus.*
Dorsal color brown or tan in adults; nasal septum with a conspicuous posterior emargination: 9

9. Hairs of throat plumbeous basally (rarely a patch of hairs white to the base); anterointernal rëentrant angle of upper M1 extending more than halfway across anterior lobe of tooth: ....
....*Neotoma mexicana.*
Hairs of throat white basally; anterointernal rëentrant angle of upper M1 extending less than halfway across anterior lobe of tooth:
....10

10. Tail with moderately long hairs, sometimes only vaguely bicolored;

lingual fold of M3 as deep as or deeper than labial fold; nasals usually truncate posteriorly: . . . .*Neotoma stephensi.*

Tail with very short hairs, always sharply bicolored; lingual fold of M3 shorter than labial fold; nasals sharply pointed posteriorly: . . . .*Neotoma albigula.*

11. Tail laterally compressed, long, scaly; condylobasal length more than 60 mm: . . . .*Ondatra zibethicus.*

    Tail rounded, hairy; condylobasal length less than 35 mm: 12

12. Cheek teeth rooted: 13

    Cheek teeth not rooted: 14

13. Dorsal color reddish: . . . .*Clethrionomys gapperi.*

    Dorsal color grayish or brownish: . . . .*Phenacomys intermedius.*

14. Tail about one-third or more of total length: *Microtus longicaudus.*

    Tail less than one-third total length: 15

15. M3 with four dentine lakes: . . . .*Microtus ochrogaster.*

    M3 with five dentine lakes: 16

16. M2 with four dentine lakes and a posterior accessory loop: . . . .*Microtus pennsylvanicus.*

    M2 with four dentine lakes but no posterior accessory loop: . . .17

17. Incisive foramina abruptly constricted posteriorly; color dark; tails of adults usually more than 35 mm: . . . .*Microtus montanus.*

    Incisive foramina broad and truncate posteriorly; color brown; tails of adults seldom attaining 35 mm: . . . .*Microtus mexicanus.*

18. Upper incisors with a groove on anterior face: . . . .*Reithrodontomys,* 19

    Upper incisors without a groove: 21

19. Occlusal pattern of last lower molar S-shaped; occipitonasal length usually more than 22 mm; dorsal color usually rich golden brown: . . . .*Reithrodontomys fulvescens.*

    Occlusal pattern of last lower molar C-shaped; occipitonasal length usually less than 21 mm; color not golden brown: 20

20. Braincase breadth less than 9.7 mm; tail relatively short (usually less than one-half total length) and with narrow, distinct dorsal stripe: . . . .*Reithrodointomys montanus.*

    Braincase breadth more than 9.6 mm; tail longer (usually more than one-half total length), often not sharply bicolored, and dorsal stripe broader: . . . .*Reithrodontomys megalotis.*

21. Occipitonasal length of skull less than 22 mm; length of head and body less than 65 mm; length of hindfoot usually less than 20 mm: . . . .*Baiomys taylori.*

Occipitonasal length of skull more than 22 mm; length of head and body more than 65 mm; length of hindfoot usually 20 mm or more: 22

22. Coronoid process relatively high and recurved; tail length less than 60 percent of length of head and body: . . . .*Onychomys*, 23
Coronoid process relatively low, not strongly recurved; tail length more than 60 percent of length of head and body: *Peromyscus*, 24

23. Tail less than half the length of head and body; crown length of maxillary tooth-row 4.0 mm or more: . . . .*Onychomys leucogaster.*
Tail more than half the length of head and body; crown length of maxillary tooth-row 3.9 mm or less: . . . .*Onychomys arenicola.*

24. Two principal labial rëentrant angles of first and second upper molars with accessory tubercles or enamel loops: 26
Two principal labial rëentrant angles of first and second upper molars without (or, at best, with rudimentary) accessory tubercles or enamel loops: 25

25. Tail well-haired and tufted; fur long and soft; nasals exceed premaxillae slightly or not at all: . . . .*Peromyscus crinitus.*
Tail with extremely short hairs, almost naked, not tufted; nasals decidedly longer than premaxillae: . . . .*Peromyscus eremicus.*

26. Tail tufted, with terminal hairs that are conspicuously longer than others: 28
Tail terete, that is, with no conspicuously elongate terminal hairs: 27

27. Hindfoot length 21 mm or less; greatest length of skull less than 27 mm; tail sharply bicolored: . . . .*Peromyscus maniculatus.*
Hindfoot length more than 21 mm; greatest length of skull more than 27 mm; tail often not sharply bicolored: *Peromyscus leucopus.*

28. Ear usually 20 mm or less: 29
Ear usually 20 mm or more: 30

29. Ankles white: . . . .*Peromyscus pectoralis.*
Extension of dark dorsal coloration extending distally over ankle: . . . .*Peromyscus boylii.*

30. Length of ear longer than length of hindfoot on fresh specimens; tail length usually shorter than head and body length: . . . .*Peromyscus truei.**
Length of ear equal to or shorter than length of hindfoot; tail usually longer than head and body length: . . . .*Peromyscus difficilis.*

---

*Recently, some populations of *P. truei* in southwestern New Mexico have been recognized as a distinct species, *P. gratus.*

31. Venter ochraceous: ....*Sigmodon fulviventer.*
    Venter not ochraceous: 32
32. Snout, eye-rings, and sometimes upper forelegs yellowish or or-
    angish, total length usually less than 260 mm: ....
    ....*S. ochrognathus.*
    Snout, eye-rings, and upper forelegs not as above; total length
    often more than 260 mm:........................*S. hispidus.*

Key to Carnivores of New Mexico

1. Total number of teeth, thirty-two or less; muzzle short and broad;
   claws rectractile:...................................Felidae, 2
   Total number of teeth, thirty-two or more; claws not rectractile, or
   only partly so: 4
2. Tail more than 30 percent of total length; three upper premolars:
   ....*Felis,* 3
   Tail less than 30 percent of total length; two upper premolars: ...
   ....*Lynx rufus.*
3. Dorsal color uniform:.............................*Felis concolor.*
   Dorsal color spotted: ....*Felis onca.*
4. Hindfoot with four toes:...........................Canidae, 5
   Hindfoot with five toes: 10
5. Postorbital process thick, convex dorsally; condylobasal length
   greater than 160 mm: ....*Canis,* 6
   Postorbital process thin, concave dorsally; condylobasal length less
   than 150 mm: 7
6. Condylobasal length usually more than 210 mm; with mandibles
   articulated and jaws closed, tips of upper canines do not usually
   reach a line connecting mental foramina:..........*Canis lupus.*
   Condylobasal length usually less than 190 mm; with mandible articulated and jaws closed, tips of upper canines extend below
   line connecting mental foramina:................*Canis latrans.*
7. Temporal ridges converge posteriorly in a U-shape; a step on ventral margin of dentary in front of angular process; a dorsal black
   stripe on tail:......................*Urocyon cinereoargenteus.*
   Temporal ridges converge posteriorly in a V-shape; no step on
   ventral margin of dentary; no dorsal black stripe on tail: 8
8. Tailtip white; posterior surface of ear pinnae black; condylobasal
   length more than 130 mm: ....*Vulpes vulpes.*
   Tailtip black; posterior surface of pinnae brownish; condylobasal
   length less than 120 mm:...............................9

9. Ear greater than 75 mm from notch; auditory bullae large:.......
....*Vulpes macrotis.*
Ear less than 75 mm from notch; auditory bullae small: ....
....*Vulpes velox.*

10. Tail shorter than hindfoot; total length of adults 1,200 mm or more; 42 or fewer teeth: ....Ursidae, 11
Tail longer than hindfoot; total length of adults less than 1,200 mm; 40 or fewer teeth:.....................................12

11. Front claws approximately same length as hind ones; no hump at shoulder; second upper molar (last tooth in row) widest near its midpoint; maxillary tooth-row less than 110 mm:.............
....*Ursus americanus.*
Front claws obviously longer than hind ones; conspicuous hump at shoulder; second upper molar widest near front; maxillary tooth-row more than 110 mm: ....*Ursus arctos.*

12. Tail usually ringed; forty teeth; no anal scent glands: ....
....Procyonidae, 13
Tail never ringed; less than forty teeth; anal scent glands present: ....Mustelidae, 15

13. Fourth upper premolar bladelike:.............*Bassariscus astutus.*
Fourth upper premolar molariform: 14

14. Basilar length of skull more than 115 mm; total length more than 1,000 mm; rostrum and snout elongate and tubular: ....
....*Nasua nasua.*
Basilar length of skull less than 115 mm; total length less than 1,000 mm; rostrum not markedly elongate or tubular: . .*Procyon lotor.*

15. Dorsal coloration black and white; posterior border of hard palate not extending appreciably behind last molars:..............16
Dorsal coloration not black and white; posterior border of hard palate extending appreciably behind last molars: 19

16. Snout with an enlarged hairless rooting area; two upper premolars on each side; total teeth, thirty-two:......*Conepatus mesoleucus.*
Snout not modified as above; three upper premolars on each side; total teeth, thirty-four: 17

17. Back with four or more lines of broken white stripes or spots; length of skull less than 60 mm:.............*Spilogale putorius.*
Back black, or with continuous white stripes; length of skull more than 60 mm: 18

18. Tail length more than that of head and body; white stripes variable, often nearly absent; bullae somewhat enlarged: ....
....*Mephitis macroura.*

Tail length less than that of head and body; white stripes usually prominent; bullae not enlarged: . . . . *Mephitis mephitis.*

19. Premolars 4/4: . . . . *Martes americana.*

    Premolars 2 to 4/3:. 20

20. Foot rounded; toes webbed; premolars 4/3; upper molar nearly square; total length more than 840 mm: . . . . *Lutra canadensis.*

    Foot not round; toes not webbed; premolars fewer than 4/3; upper molar not square:. 21

21. Body stout; white stripe on head; foreclaws 30 mm or longer; condylobasal length more than 110 mm: . . . . *Taxidea taxus.*

    Body slender; no white stripe on head; foreclaws less than 20 mm; condylobasal length less than 80 mm: 22

22. Hindfoot greater than 55 mm; condylobasal length greater than 60 mm:. 23

    Hindfoot less than 50 mm; condylobasal length less than 55 mm: 24

23. Color of body and tail yellowish; tip of tail, facemask, and feet black:. . . . . *Mustela nigripes.*

    Color uniformly medium to dark brown; tail, face, and feet not distinctively colored: . . . . *Mustela vison.*

24. Venter white to sulphur-yellow in summer; condylobasal length less than 35 mm:. . . . . *Mustela erminea.*

    Venter orangish brown in summer; condylobasal length more than 40 mm: . . . . *Mustela frenata.*

Key to Hooved Animals of New Mexico

1. Upper incisors present; body shape piglike; elongate canines:. . . . . *Tayassu tajacu.*

    No upper incisors; body shape not piglike; canines absent, or if present, not elongate:. 2

2. Males with antlers (females without antlers or horns); a large antorbital fenestra; lateral digits present: . . . . .Cervidae, 6

    Males and females with horns (a bony frontal core covered with a keratinized sheath); large antorbital fenestra absent, or if present, lateral digits lacking or vestigial:. 3

3. Horns forked; antorbital fenestra present; lateral digits absent or vestigial:. . . . . *Antilocapra americana.*

    Horns not forked; antorbital fenestra absent; four hooves (including two vestigial hooves) on each foot: .4

4. Horns smooth and anterodorsally directed; cow-sized; dark brown
   in color: . . . . *Bison bison.*
   Horns with annular ridges, posteriorly curved; sheep-sized: 5
5. Males with midventral mane of hair on neck: . .*Ammotragus lervia.*
   Males without midventral mane on neck: . . . .*Ovis canadensis.*
6. Antlers with a prominent brow tine; upper canines present; vomer
   not attached to medial suture of palatines, not separating posterior narial cavity; prominent yellow rump patch:. . . . .
   . . . .*Cervus elaphus.*
   Antlers without prominent brow tine; upper canines absent; vomer
   attached to medial suture of palatines, completely separating
   narial cavity; no large yellow rump patch: 7
7. Tail white, tipped with black tuft; antlers branched dichotomously,
   anterior and posterior beams nearly equal:. . . . .
   . . . .*Odocoileus hemionus.*
   Tail white below, brown above; antlers with one main anteriorly
   directed beam with smaller tines branching dorsally from it:. . .
   . . . .*Odocoileus virginianus.*

Marsupials

ORDER MARSUPIALIA

Marsupials are mammals which bear their young at a very early stage of development, when they are little more than embryos. The babies then spend a substantial period of development in a fur-lined pouch located on the ventral surface of the mother, where they attach themselves firmly to her nipples. Not all marsupials have a pouch like that of a kangaroo; some have only folds of skin which cover the young. All marsupials are characterized also by a suite of cranial characteristics. Most marsupials are found in the Australian region, and many are also found in the New World tropics. The common opossum is the only species currently found in the United States. At one time there were many more kinds of marsupials in South America, including some that resembled saber-toothed cats, and others that were not unlike modern kangaroo rats. Most of these kinds became extinct soon after South America became connected to North America by the Central American land bridge several million years ago. Most of the marsupials remaining in the New World are opposumlike or shrewlike animals.

Virginia Opossum

Didelphis virginiana. The opossum is a cat-sized, long-furred, gray animal with large pink and white naked ears and a long naked tail of the same color. The snout is long and tapering, and the face, seen in the headlights of a car at night, appears as white. Each foot is provided with five toes, and the first toe on the hindfoot is opposable. The tail is prehensile and may be used as an aid in climbing. Female opossums are provided with a fur-lined pouch on the ventral surface of the body, in which the young are sheltered.

Only a few opossums have been detected in New Mexico, in Bernalillo, Quay and Hidalgo counties. In the West, opossums seem partial to humid areas, and a few may live in the Rio Grande or Pecos valleys or perhaps in other agricultural areas. There is evidence from Colorado that the animals have been moving westward since about 1930, and some of our records may be comprised of these relatively recent immigrants. On the other hand, the species has been introduced into Arizona, California, and other parts of the Far West, where it was not native; and it is possible that some have been released in New Mexico.

Opossums can climb, but spend much time on the ground and seek shelter in a variety of places, including the burrows of other mammals. When attacked, the opossum may enter a catatonic state in which it will appear to be lifeless. There is no detectable change in its heart rate, however, and after a few minutes the animal revives. Most kinds of food are consumed, although animal food is generally preferred.

Once or twice a year, females may produce up to twenty-five young. The babies are born after a gestation of only thirteen days, and they make their way unaided into the pouch of the female, where they attach themselves to a nipple and remain until about seventy days old. Young opossums show little play behavior, and the female gives them scant care. Except for the brief association of the male and female during mating, opossums have no social life.

Opossums are hunted for human food, and the fur is rather commonly used.

Insectivores

Insectivores are mostly small, nocturnal, sharp-nosed, small-eyed mammals which feed on insects and other small animals. In the New World, the order is represented by shrews and moles, and by the rare solenodon of Cuba and Haiti. In the Old World, shrews and moles are present; and hedgehogs, otter shrews, elephant shrews, tenrecs, golden moles, and tree shrews are often grouped in this category. There is considerable doubt, however, that all of these diverse animals are really closely related, and one view is that they resemble one another merely because they have all retained many features characteristic of primitive placental mammals. There seems to be little doubt, however, that the New World kinds are related.

SHREWS

Family Soricidae

There are eight kinds of shrews known to live in Mexico. All are very small. The dwarf shrew may weigh so little as 2 grams, and is one of the smallest mammals known. The largest species in the state, the water shrew, may weigh 20 grams and attain a head and body length of 100 mm (4 inches) but is still a very small animal. Shrews are mouselike in proportions, but differ from mice in their elongate, pointed muzzles,

31

and in their tiny eyes. The ears also tend to be small and partially hidden in their fur. Each foot is provided with five toes.

Because of their small size, shrews lose a lot of heat through the body surface, which is large in proportion to the volume of the animal. To make up for this loss, shrews must spend a great deal of their time in hunting and eating. As a result, they are quite active and are aggressive predators, consuming large quantities of small invertebrates such as insects, earthworms, and spiders, and occasionally even a vertebrate or two. It has been found that a shrew may often consume food equal to or exceeding its own weight in a twenty-four-hour period. Shrews also drink readily and are commonly found in the vicinity of water.

Some female shrews may reach sexual maturity at the age of two months, but in New Mexico the growing season is so short in most places where shrews live that a female born in June or July does not bear a litter until the following year. In some places, shrews do have more than one litter a year, but we have not yet observed this in our state. Four or five young comprise a brood. The babies are born in a small nest lined with plant material or hair that is placed under a log or rock or a similarly secure shelter. The infants are naked and blind at birth, but mature rapidly. Although the young may remain with the mother for a short while after emerging from the nest, there is little evidence of any other kind of social life for these little creatures.

Shrews hunt by day and night, foraging under leaves, grass, sticks, and logs in the forest, and under other sorts of cover. Because of this and because they move so quickly, they are seldom observed. Prey is probably located by a combination of scent and hearing. Probably all shrews produce high frequency cries, above the range of human hearing, which then echo back to the animal and provide information about the environment. There is also some evidence that shrews may travel on habitual paths that they traverse by memory. Probably all can swim to some extent, but the water shrew, which is common in the mountains of northern New Mexico, can swim with great facility, diving under water to pursue aquatic organisms, and even running across the surface for short distances. A few shrews produce a mild poison which subdues the small animals upon which they prey, but this has not been found to be the case for any of the New Mexican kinds.

Shrews are preyed upon regularly by owls and hawks, and have been found in the stomachs of a variety of other predators such as snakes, foxes, and skunks. However, some of these animals have been observed to reject shrews in preference to other kinds of food. Since many shrews have scent-producing glands on their flanks or ventral surfaces, it has been suggested that many kinds of potential predators find them unpalatable.

In those communities where they are common, shrews are important predators on smaller animals, and thus play a part in the cycling of materials through the ecosystem. None of our local species have been shown to have any special economic importance to man.

The montane shrew (*Sorex monticolus*) is probably the most common and widespread species in the state. It is found in montane forests of most of the larger mountain ranges, and seems to prefer moist streamside meadows. Also common is the water shrew (*Sorex palustris*), which, however, seems to be limited to the Jemez, San Juan, and Sangre de Cristo mountains, where it lives along permanent streams. At lower elevations, in deserts and grasslands, the desert shrew (*Notiosorex crawfordi*) occurs in sites that provide a humid microclimate, such as boulder fields or marshy areas along the Rio Grande. In some places, this unusual desert-adapted shrew has been found living in the nests of pack rats and in beehives. The remaining species of shrews are much less commonly encountered, either because they are rare or because mammalogists have not yet figured out exactly where they live and how to capture them. The masked shrew (*Sorex cinereus*) is limited to the higher, wetter areas of the northern mountains. The Merriam shrew (*Sorex merriami*) and the dwarf shrew (*Sorex nanus*) are presently known from so few sites that it is difficult to generalize about their habitat requirements. The former seems widespread in drier forests and woodlands, and the latter may have a preference for rock slides in forested areas. The least shrew (*Cryptotis parva*), a species that is common in the central grasslands of the United States, has recently been discovered living in a marsh near Tucumcari. The greatest rarity on the roster of New Mexican shrews is the Arizona shrew (*Sorex arizonae*). This southern species has only recently been made known to science, and so far has been detected only on a few mountains in Arizona, northern Mexico, and the Animas Mountains of Hidalgo County, New Mexico.

Identification of shrews is difficult, even for a specialist. Except for the water shrew, which is easily recognized by its striking black and white coloration, shrews are very similar externally, and certain identification is dependent upon examination of the upper teeth with a hand lens or microscope. Between the large hooked upper incisor and the broad complicated premolar is a row of small, single-cusped teeth called unicuspids. These unicuspids vary in size; some may be so small that they can be seen only by looking straight down on the palate of the skull with a dissecting microscope. *Notiosorex* has three unicuspids; *Cryptotis* has four; all the *Sorex* have five. *Sorex merriami* and *S. arizonae* differ from all the other species of *Sorex* in that the unicuspids do not have a darkly pigmented ridge extending from the tip of the tooth toward the palate, ending in a small cusplet, and both species have two miniscule holes on the inside of the back end of the lower jawbone (a mandibular and a postmandibular foramen). *Sorex arizonae* has a small medial tine on each upper incisor, and *S. merriami* lacks these tines. The remaining species of *Sorex* have the medially directed pigmented ridges and cusplets on the upper unicuspids, and lack the posteriormost of the two holes mentioned above (the postmandibular foramen). *Sorex cinereus* differs from *nanus, monticolus,* and *palustris* in that its unicuspids grade uniformly from large in front to small in back. The other three have the third unicuspid (counting from the front) smaller than the fourth. *Sorex palustris* differs because of its large size and the black and white two-toned pelage. *Sorex monticolus* is much like *nanus,* but it is larger: total length usually measures 100 millimeters or more, and the skull is more than 15 mm in length. In addition, the braincase of *S. nanus* is very flat. That of *S. monticolus* is more arched.

MOLES

Family Talpidae

No moles have ever been detected within the state of New Mexico. The burrowing animals that leave mounds on ditch banks, in alfalfa fields, in mountain meadows, in gardens, and in other places are pocket gophers, that is, rodents of the family Geomyidae.

Nonetheless, biologists continue to keep an eye out for the presence of moles in some part of the state, for the eastern mole (*Scalopus aquaticus*) has been found very close to our borders: in the trans-Pecos region of Texas, and near the Cimarron River in Baca County, southeastern Colorado. If you find a rat-sized black animal with velvety fur, no eyes, a pointed nose, and broad, flat, enlarged front feet, take it to the nearest naturalist for a certain identification: you may have discovered the state's first mole!

Bats

There are twenty-five kinds of bats in New Mexico, and in some parts of the state they are very common during the warm months. All of our species are rather small. The smallest is the western pipistrelle which weighs about 5 to 6 grams, while the largest is probably the mastiff bat, weighing 60 grams. Truly large bats are found only in tropical and subtropical regions. Our bats are mostly colored drab shades of brown, black, and gray. However, the hoary and red bats have variegated fur tipped with white, and one of the most spectacularly colored bats in the world is the spotted bat, a black and white animal with three large white spots on a black background dorsally, with enormous pink ears.

With only a few known exceptions, New Mexican bats feed upon insects and other small invertebrates. The pallid bat (*Antrozous pallidus*) is known to land on the ground and capture lizards and scorpions, and the two state species in the leaf-nosed bat family are specialized for a diet of nectar.

Between August, or September, and April few bats are seen in New Mexico. Most species hibernate, while a few kinds are known to migrate to more southern places. Curiously enough, few winter retreats (hibernacula) have been found in our state.

Bats find their way about in the dark by means of echolocation, a process of producing very high frequency cries, the echoes of which return from obstacles or from flying insects and inform the bat of its surroundings. These cries are usually above the range of human hearing, that is, greater than twenty thousand cycles per second. A few bats produce echolocation calls that can be heard by most people. Bats with their ears or their mouths blocked soon become disoriented and either land or fall to the ground.

The bats living in our region mate and produce young but once a year; and most produce only a single baby. Mating most commonly takes place in the fall, while the bats are gathering at their hibernacula or while they are en route to winter quarters. In some species, copulation occurs during brief periods of arousal from hibernation, or after emergence in the spring. From fall matings the sperm are stored in the vagina or uterus of the female until spring. Then, when the female arouses from hibernation, ovulation and fertilization take place. For most species, the gestation period is two to three months. The young are blind and helpless and totally dependent upon the mother until, at three or four weeks of age, they take wing and begin to forage for themselves. After the young become volant they are essentially adult size. Bats—like many birds, but unlike many other small mammals—grow very little after they leave their natal shelter.

Bats have few natural predators. A few are captured by hawks and owls, and some are captured in their roosts by snakes or mammalian predators. Much bat mortality is attributable to human activity. Pesticides, such as DDT, seem to accumulate in bats because they ingest the poison along with their insect prey. Some of these pesticides seem to be stored in the fat that some bats accumulate before migration. Then, when the fat reserves are utilized during the migratory flight, the bats are killed by the pesticides. Many bats spend an important part of their life cycle in caves or caverns. Such places have a great attraction for humans, too; and many bats are killed by people, or driven from their shelter never to return. It has been shown that these shelters are one of the most important limiting resources for many kinds of bats. When the shelters are denied to them, the bats disappear from the region. Given that most bats are insect feeders, the consequences of bat destruction for ecosystems in general, and for human ecosystems in particular, may be far reaching.

Many kinds of bats have been found occasionally to be infected with rabies. The bite of a rabid bat can transmit the virus to other animals, including humans. Rabid bats are often lethargic and easily captured. There are even a few cases in which a rabid bat has deliberately attacked a human. Such occurrences are extremely rare, however, and chances are slight that anyone will encounter a rabid bat, much less contract the disease. Yet it is a good idea to refrain from handling bats, especially if their behavior is unusual. In the event that you are bitten by a bat, the animal should be taken to the State Public Health Laboratory for examination, and you should consult a physician.

Bats sometimes choose to live in houses or in other man-made structures, especially during the migratory season in the fall. Bats arriving in the fall to roost on porches, in garages, or in barns will usually be gone in a week or two. If a colony of bats decides to use your house in the summer, you may find yourself annoyed by the noise or odor. About the only defense is to find where the bats are entering and make an effort to deny them access. Fumigation is rarely effective. If the bats are in a building where no harm results from their presence, they should be left alone. A small colony of mother brown bats, feeding their babies in June or July, will consume an enormous volume of flying insects.

New Mexican bats belong to one of three families. Leaf-nosed bats (family Phyllostomatidae) are recognizable by the presence of a triangular flap of skin rising from the tip of the snout. Only two kinds have been found in New Mexico, all in Hidalgo County, where they are limited in distribution and uncommon. Freetail bats (family Molossidae) have a long, mouselike tail, which protrudes a considerable distance behind the flight membrane stretching between the tail and the hind legs. Four kinds occur in the state, including the famous Brazilian free-tailed bat, which inhabits Carlsbad Caverns in large numbers. Most New Mexican bats belong to the common bat family, Vespertilionidae. These bats present a variety of different appearances, but none has a nose leaf, and none has a free tail.

LEAF-NOSED BATS

Family Phyllostomatidae

Leaf-nosed bats are limited to the New World, where they are found mostly in the tropics. Two species enter Hidalgo County in the summer: the long-tongued bat (*Choeronycteris mexicana*), and the long-nosed bat (*Leptonycteris sanborni*). Both have a long, slender snout and a nose leaf. *Choeronycteris* is distinctive in possessing a short but visible tail, which *Leptonycteris* lacks. *Choeronycteris* has three upper and three lower molar teeth, while *Leptonycteris* has but two. Finally, *Choeronycteris* lacks a complete zygomatic arch (cheekbone), while that of *Leptonycteris* is complete.

Both species belong to a group of leaf-nosed bats which are specialized for feeding upon nectar and perhaps pollen. The specializations include the long snout and a very long protrusible tongue covered at the end with bottle-brush-like bristles that allow the animal to withdraw nectar from flowers. Both species, unlike many bats, have the ability to hover in one place while feeding. These animals might be regarded ecologically as nocturnal hummingbirds. Like hummingbirds, they are known to be instrumental in pollinating flowers. In New Mexico, it is probable that the summer arrival of the animals coincides with the blooming of century plants (agaves) and perhaps yuccas as well. Probably, both species bring forth their young within our borders. Young flower bats are somewhat more developed at birth than other New Mexican species.

FREE-TAILED BATS

Family Molossidae

Free-tailed bats are found throughout the world in tropical and subtropical regions. Four species have been detected in New Mexico. Most free-tailed bats have long slender wings and are specialized for fast, long-distance flight. The hind legs are not as reduced as they are in other bats; for example, both shank bones, the tibia and fibula, are well developed, and the bats are capable of rapid quadrupedal locomotion. The ears of molossids incline forward and laterally, and may even provide some lift for the bat when it is in flight. Free-tailed bats are known to make extensive foraging flights. The Brazilian free-tailed bat of Carlsbad may disperse from the cave in flocks that fly at an altitude of nine thousand feet, and may cover fifty miles to the foraging grounds. The mastif bat has been recorded spending as much as six hours aloft in a single foraging flight. When returning to roost, a free-tailed bat may dive at great speed from a high altitude, pulling up at the last minute to enter the shelter. While in flight, some free-tailed bats probably communicate with each other vocally, producing loud chirps that are audible to humans.

Our species leave the state in winter, except for a few Brazilian free-tails. The females are pregnant when the bats return in April. Males and females may segregate, with the females forming maternity colonies and the males forming smaller bachelor groups. After the young leave the roost, the autumnal migration begins, and most individuals are gone by November. It is during the fall migration that numbers build up in roosts of transients. In this season, the bats are most apt to be found in buildings.

Of the New Mexican kinds, the Brazilian free-tailed bat (*Tadarida brasiliensis*) is by far the most common. Large numbers inhabit Carlsbad Caverns, both during the breeding and migratory seasons. A few have been known to spend the winter there, although most migrate to central and southern Mexico. In the caves and caverns where these animals roost, there appear huge accumulations of fecal pellets, known as guano. The guano has a commercial value as fertilizer, and it has been mined in many areas. Although the guano is useful, the work of the guano miners has often resulted in the destruction of valuable archaeological deposits in the caves as well as rendering the shelters unsuitable for further occupany by the bats. The big free-tailed bat (*Nyctinomops* [formerly *Tadarida*] *macrotis*) is much less common. It is known from a few small summer roosts in sandstone and lava cliffs. Its habits are little known. The pocketed free-tailed bat (*N.* [formerly *Tadarida*] *femorosacca*) has been detected in New Mexico only at Carlsbad and in Hidalgo County. While rare in our state, this species is common in southern Arizona. The mastif bat (*Eumops perotis*) is probably the largest bat known from the United States. In this country it is known from southern Arizona and California; occasionally, it enters Hidalgo County, New Mexico. This may be one of the strongest fliers among our species, cruising over hundreds of miles of desert terrain in search of flying insects.

Among New Mexican free-tailed bats, *Eumops* is distinctive because its lips lack the vertical folds or pleats which distinguish the lips of *Tadarida* and *Nyctinomops*. Furthermore, it is the largest of our free-tailed bats, possessing a forearm that measures more than 65 millimeters in length. *Tadarida* differs from *Nyctinomops* in that its ears are not joined together where they approach each other on the forehead, the second joint in its fourth finger is more than 5 millimeters long, and its forearm measures less than 45 millimeters. The ears of *Nyctinomops* are fused together over the forehead, the second joint of the fourth finger is less than 5 millimeters, and the forearm is greater than 45 millimeters in length. Of the two, *Nyctinomops femorosacca* is smaller: its forearm is less than 55 millimeters and its skull is less than 21 millimeters long. *N. macrotis* has a forearm which exceeds 55 millimeters, and a skull greater than 21 millimeters in length.

COMMON BATS

Family Vespertilionidae

Most New Mexican bats belong to this family. Vespertilionid bats are quite diverse in appearance and habits, but none has a nose leaf, and none has a free tail. Unlike free-tailed bats, which seem to be best at high-speed, long-distance foraging, vespertilionids seem capable of highly maneuverable flight, often in cluttered habitats. Using sophisticated frequency-modulated sonar, a vespertilionid can close rapidly on an erratically fleeing insect, capturing it in the mouth with the tail membrane, or even with the wing membrane. Some vespertilionids are more like molossids in foraging behavior—for example, the tree bats of the genus *Lasiurus*. But others are masters of slow, controlled flight in crowded spaces—for example, the big-eared bat (*Plecotus*) or the fringed myotis (*Myotis thysanodes*). Common bats may seek shelter in caves, human habitations, hollow trees or under their bark, rock shelters, rock crevices, or even beneath rocks on the ground. A few species, such as the tree bats of the genus *Lasiurus*, may rest in the open, hanging in the foliage of trees. These animals emerge to forage soon after sundown. For an hour or two they may be incredibly active in their pursuit of prey. Then they may seek a temporary shelter—known as a night roost— where they rest and digest their meal. After capturing a large item, some species may hang up to consume the prey. Late in the night, many species take wing again for a feeding bout of lesser intensity than the first one, and afterward they seek daytime shelter. During the day, some bats allow their body temperatures to drop, thus conserving energy. This may be especially true in late summer, when the saved energy accumulates as fat to be used during migration or hibernation. Except for tree bats, female vespertilionids in our state tend to get together in the spring to share a roost—called a maternity roost—where the babies are brought forth. These roosts are found generally in places where the young, at first unable to maintain their body temperatures, may stay warm enough to grow rapidly. When the female is about to give birth, she assumes a head-up position, and the newly emerged baby is caught in her tail membrane. Babies are sometimes carried by their mothers on foraging flights, but more often they are left in the roost when the females emerge to hunt. When the youngsters first take wing, their attempts at hunting must be rather inefficient, but they quickly become adept. Each young bat must then accumulate enough food reserves to fly to its wintering quarters, and then to hibernate through the winter.

This is a very demanding task, and it is probably this first late summer and the ensuing winter that results in most of the mortality suffered among the young. If the bat is successful in surviving its first hibernation, its chances of a fairly long life are quite good. Vespertilionid bats have a long life expectancy for animals of such small size; up to twenty-four years has been confirmed for *Myotis lucifugus*. While females are rearing the young, the males may live a solitary life or exist with small numbers of other males, quite apart from the females. In hibernation, the bat's temperature may drop to a few degrees above freezing. However, the bat warms and revives somewhat on a regular basis. During the summer, male bats produce sperm, but by the time the animals head for the winter quarters the testes have become inactive and the sperm are stored in the long coiled tubes called epididymides. The sperm may be used in matings before hibernation, but remain viable throughout the winter and can be used in matings in the spring. For females mated in the fall, the sperm remain alive in the uterus until spring.

Nineteen kinds of vespertilionids have been recorded from New Mexico. Some, like the spotted bat (*Euderma*) and the hoary and red bats (*Lasiurus*), are readily recognized; but many of the species are undistinguished in appearance, resembling one another to the extent that careful examination of teeth, measurements, and other anatomical features is necessary for accurate identification. Our vespertilionids may be grouped into three fairly recognizable categories for identification purposes. All tree bats, genera *Lasiurus* and *Lasionycteris,* have a covering of hair over at least half of the top surface of the flight membrane, which extends between the hind legs and the tail (the uropatagium). On most of them, this membrane is completely furred. These bats tend to have short rounded ears. All long-eared bats, genera *Antrozous, Plecotus, Idionycteris,* and *Euderma,* have truly enormous ears, which reach far beyond the tip of the nose if they are laid forward. The remaining bats, genera *Myotis, Eptesicus,* and *Pipistrellus,* have neither the furred uropatagium nor the huge ears.

Lasiurus differs from *Lasionycteris* in possessing one pair of upper incisor teeth rather than two pairs. These teeth may be viewed between the long upper canines in the front of the mouth.

Among the big-eared bats, the spotted bat (*Euderma maculatum*) is readily distinguishable because of its striking color pattern. The animal is black dorsally with three white spots, and is white ventrally with a black collar. *Idionycteris* may be identified by the presence of a pair of small rounded flaps of skin called lappets, which are found between the ears at the point where they join over the forehead. *Antrozous* differs from *Plecotus* in having one pair of upper incisors, rather than two, and in its yellowish white coloration, rather than a hue of dull brown or gray.

Myotis differs from *Eptesicus* and *Pipistrellus* in the possession of a sharp-pointed flap of skin (the tragus), which extends vertically from the lower margin of the ear opening. The other two genera have a tragus, but its tip is blunt and rounded rather than sharp. Finally, *Eptesicus* differs from *Pipistrellus* in much larger size: its forearm measures 39 millimeters or more in length, as opposed to 35 or less in *Pipistrellus*. *Eptesicus* is brown; *Pipistrellus* is yellowish. Finally, *Pipistrellus* has one tiny (premolar) tooth between the upper canine and the first large complex tooth of the upper tooth row; *Eptesicus* has no such tiny tooth.

TREE BATS

Genus *Lasiurus*

Since these bats roost in the open, they tend to have more and denser fur than many other kinds. The dorsal surface of the tail membrane is furred, and the wrists and ears—exposed places from which heat may be lost—also have coverings of hair. Unlike most other vespertilionids, *Lasiurus* tends to be solitary, with the only exception being the cluster formed by the female and her babies during the season of reproduction. The fur of *Lasiurus* has been shown to have greater insulative properties than the fur of other common bats. Moreover, these animals seem more resistant to cold and to water loss, characteristics of obvious adaptive value in a bat that roosts in exposed places. Red bats and hoary bats (*L. borealis* and *L. cinereus*) are presumed to be migratory. Red bats are known to hibernate while hanging in trees, and they have the ability to arouse after the body temperature has dropped so low as −3° C. Both red and hoary bats are occasionally found in caves, but it is thought that they do not regularly hibernate in such places. Mating probably takes place during the fall migration. A few observations suggest that copulation occurs while the animals are in flight. The curiously spined penis of the male may act as a locking device to hold the pair together until ejaculation is completed. When female red and hoary bats return to New Mexico in the spring they are pregnant, carrying from one to five young. However, the expectant-mother hoary bats do not loiter in the state, continuing on to the eastern part of the country to give birth. Males may remain in the higher mountains of

New Mexico throughout the summer. Female red bats, however, stay in the southern part of the state to raise their youngsters, while males are scarce within our borders.

Three kinds of *Lasiurus* occur in the state: the hoary bat (*Lasiurus cinereus*), the red bat (*L. borealis*), and the yellow bat (*L. ega*). The latter is the most sparsely furred of the three, having only about the front half of the uropatagium covered with hair. *L. ega* is yellowish, hence its common name. *L. borealis* is reddish, and *cinereus* is grayish. Finally, the latter two species possess a minute peglike premolar tooth in each upper tooth-row, located medially in the angle between the canine and the first large complex tooth (the fourth premolar). Of course, this tiny tooth can only be seen after microscopic examination of a properly cleaned skull. The red and hoary bat are quite different in size as well as in color. The hoary is the larger of the two, with a forearm always exceeding 49 millimeters. Red bats are smaller, with forearms always less than 49 millimeters.

Red bats have been found only in the southern part of the state, and probably prefer gallery forests or woodlands along watercourses. Hoary bats have been observed statewide during migration. The yellow bat has been recorded only in Hidalgo County.

Silver-Haired Bat

Lasionycteris noctivagans.   Like *Lasiurus,* silver-haired bats are considered to be tree bats. However, records of tree-roosting in this species seem to be rare. Indeed, few of these bats have been found in their daytime shelters. Some have been detected under the bark of dead trees, in buildings, and in fissures in rock ledges. In New Mexico, silver-haired bats are most common during June when most of the animals captured are males. Females are captured in smaller numbers in early spring, and again in late fall when they are found to have been inseminated. The evidence thus suggests that the females may go elsewhere to bear their young. The usual number of young for this species is two. These bats have been found hibernating in caves in the east, but there are no winter records for New Mexico. In summer the species is most common high in the mountains, but during migration the animals may be found at any altitude. Indeed, migrating flocks of silver-haired bats have been seen far out at sea.

Big Brown Bat

Eptesicus fuscus.   This is one of the most common bats in New Mexico in forested areas, especially in the ponderosa pine zone. During migration to winter quarters, individuals may be found at any altitude. A few have been found hibernating in mines near Albuquerque. In summer these animals shelter in hollow trees, under bark, in rock fissures, under bridges, and in buildings. *Eptesicus* is one of the earliest bats to take flight in the mountains, and may be seen foraging while it is still light. While a variety of flying insects are consumed, this species seems to have a preference for beetles. Mating takes place in the fall. In New Mexico, females bear a single young in spring; however, in the eastern part of the country, two young are the rule. Animals of both sexes may attain sexual maturity at the end of their first summer.

Western Pipistrelle

Pipistrellus hesperus. These tiny bats are chiefly inhabitants of deserts and grasslands, although a few are seen at slightly higher elevations. An important requirement for this species seems to be the presence of rocky areas in the vicinity of a water source. The bats seek shelter among rocks, and seem not to fly great distances to seek water. In the proper place, pipistrelles may literally fill the air during their early evening foraging and watering period. Pipistrelles hibernate, probably in the same areas where they spend the summer, though there are few definite winter records. In New Mexico, these bats have been found hiding under flat stones on the ground. Females bear one or more, commonly two, babies.

LITTLE BROWN BATS

Genus *Myotis*

Nine species of little brown bats occur in New Mexico. All are quite similar in appearance and are sometimes difficult even for experts to identify. The various species tend to have different habitat preferences, or to occupy different parts of the state. Nonetheless, in some favored sites in the central mountains five or six species commonly occur together. All the species are feeders on flying insects, but the manner and place of foraging may vary considerably. Three general feeding–foraging categories have been recognized in New Mexico: water-surface foragers (*M. lucifugus, M. velifer,* and *M. yumanensis*); hovering gleaners (*M. evotis, M. auriculus,* and *M. thysanodes*); and aerial pursuers (*M. californicus, M. leibii,* and *M. volans*). Members of the first group commonly forage over streams and ponds, skimming low over the water and perhaps picking up fallen insects from the surface. These water bats are almost always found where there are fairly large open bodies of water. Gleaners usually feed by picking their prey from the surface of foliage, tree trunks, rocks, or even from the ground. A gleaning bat may fly slowly and deliberately around a shrub, searching for emerging moths, or perhaps even nonflying prey. Aerial pursuers typically fly back and forth on foraging beats in clearings or in other uncluttered places, capturing flying insects which they may bag with their flight membranes or mouths. Members of the three groups are not totally limited to these methods of feeding, however, and probably each species is capable of performing in all three modes to some extent.

Members of the aerial pursuit group are distinguished by the presence of a small cartilaginous flap called a keel, which protrudes posteriorly from the trailing edge of the tail membrane. More specifically, there is a thin rod of cartilage, which supports the edge of the tail membrane, extending from the ankle of the bat toward its tail. This rod is called the calcar. The keel extends posteriorly from this calcar a short distance from the ankle, and is most easily seen in a fresh specimen. None of the other *Myotis* have the keel. Of the three species in this group, *M. volans* is distinguished from the other two in its thin covering of hair on the ventral wing membrane extending from the side of the body to about the level of the elbow. *M. volans* is quite common in montane forests. The other two species lack this hair pattern, but they are quite similar to each other, and can be distinguished with certainty only by making careful measurements of the cleaned skull. *Myotis californicus* tends to be a desert–grassland inhabitant and to occur mostly west of the Rio Grande and south of Interstate 40. *Myotis leibii* is more widespread, is often found in montane forests, and is occasionally found hibernating in caves and mineshafts.

Members of the water-bat group lack the keeled calcar and have relatively short ears that barely reach beyond the tip of the snout if they are laid forward. Distinguishing between these three requires careful study of cleaned skulls. *M. lucifugus* is often reddish in color and tends to be found along the major rivers or in certain mountain areas. *M. yumanensis* is somewhat smaller and tends to be paler in color, buffy or yellowish rather than reddish. It is almost always found near streams at lower elevations. *Myotis velifer* is most common in the drainage basin of the lower Pecos River, near the San Francisco or Gila rivers, or in southern Hidalgo County. All three of these species tend to form large maternity colonies in man-made structures or in caves. The Yuma myotis occupies the buildings of the Bosque del Apache Federal Wildlife

Refuge in large numbers, and is one of the commonest bats seen foraging over the waters there. *Myotis velifer* is often found inhabiting caves
in the limestone region of southeastern New Mexico.

The gleaning *Myotis* lack a keel, and all have very long ears which
extend appreciably beyond the tip of the muzzle when they are laid
forward. The most readily distinguished is *Myotis thysanodes*, which
has a distinct fringe of short hairs on the trailing edge of the tail membrane on either side of the tail. The other two species lack a readily
seen fringe, although they may have a few hairs which show up best
under magnification. *Myotis thysanodes* tends to occur at lower elevations, and although it may be found in lower mountains, it is most
common from the piñon-juniper zone down into the desert. The other
two species are more difficult to separate, but fortunately they have
almost mutually exclusive ranges. *Myotis evotis* has very black ears and
is most common in the mountains of northern New Mexico. *Myotis
auriculus* has brown ears, and is most common in the mountains of
central western and southwestern New Mexico. In certain west central
ranges, such as the San Mateo and Mogollon mountains and the Black
Range, both species occur, and may usually be told apart by ear color.
There is some evidence that the two species have slightly different
diets in those places where they coexist: *M. auriculus* prefers moths,
while *M. evotis* eats beetles. Where the two species occur by themselves, their diets are similar. *Myotis thysanodes* has been found in caves
and buildings. *M. auriculus* has been found night-roosting in caves.
Little is known about the roosting habits of *M. evotis*.

Spotted Bat

Euderma maculatum.   For many years after it was first made known
to science in 1891, few mammalogists encountered this species. In fact,
no scientist captured any of them in nature until Denny Constantine of
the U.S. Public Health Service netted two near Ghost Ranch in 1960.
Subsequently, a number have been captured in New Mexico, Texas, and
Utah; and they have been observed, detected by ear, or captured, from
British Columbia to Durango. Still, little information about most aspects
of the natural history of this animal have been recorded. As a result of its
seeming rarity, the species has been placed in the "rare" category on the
U.S. Fish and Wildlife Service's list of Rare and Endangered Species, and
is listed in the Red Data Book of the International Union for the Conservation of Nature. Although the animals are rarely captured by bat
collectors using mist nets set over water holes, the presence of the

animals has been detected in some places by virtue of the fact that its voice is loud and distinctive. A recent survey based on listening posts resulted in few "hearings" throughout western North America. The bats may indeed be rare; or they may vocalize only under certain circumstances; or they may have habits which make it unlikely for them to enter bat nets. The species has been found to fly much later than most bats, with many entering nets after midnight when field workers may have ceased operations for the night.

By preference, spotted bats seek shelter in rock crevices. The animals have been observed in montane forests, in woodlands, and in desert situations. Most of the food items identified have been moths; however, the bats also have been observed landing on the ground and capturing terrestrial prey. Females bear a single youngster, probably in June.

Mexican Big-Eared Bat

Idionycteris phyllotis.   These bats are commoner than spotted bats in New Mexico but seemingly occupy a narrower geographic range, for all records come from the mountains of the southwestern part of the state. Most captures have been made in ponderosa pine forest, but a few come from lower elevations. Probably *Idionycteris* roosts in rocky sites. Maternity colonies have been found in caves and rock shelters in Arizona. Males may live separately from females during the season of childrearing. A single young seems to be the rule. Food consists chiefly of moths, which may be gleaned from vegetation; but a variety of other insects is also taken.

Townsend's Big-Eared Bat

Plecotus townsendii.   Plecotus is much commoner than the previous two species of big-eared bats. Although it is uncommon for these animals to enter bat nets, they are frequently found in mines and caves. *Plecotus townsendii* is the only New Mexican bat that is regularly found in hibernation in the state. It has been suggested that these bats do not travel far, spending the winter and summer in the same general vicinity. Females form maternity colonies in the warm parts of caves or in buildings. Females mate in fall or during hibernation, and each bears a single baby in the following spring. Food consists mostly of small moths, but various other insects are also consumed. Like other big-eared bats, *Plecotus* probably takes a certain proportion of its food through gleaning.

Pallid Bat

Antrozous pallidus. This species, together with *Pipistrellus* and *Tadarida,* forms an important part of the bat fauna of New Mexico's grasslands and deserts. Pallid bats are found in such habitats practically throughout the state; although in the eastern grasslands, where shelters are less common, they are rarely found. In summer, *Antrozous* may be found roosting in buildings and in warm rock shelters and caves. The animals emerge early in the evening and forage over the desert surface, occasionally landing to capture terrestrial invertebrates (even scorpions on occasion) and small vertebrates, such as lizards and pocket mice. Of all New Mexican bats, this species is the one most adapted to the desert. Its kidneys are modified to conserve water, and captive animals have lived for a month or more with no water whatsoever. Pallid bats are quite social and generally occur in fairly large colonies. Like many other bats, females form maternity colonies; but among this species, males are often found in or near the maternity colonies. The average number of young recorded for New Mexico is about one, although as many as three babies have been recorded. Presumably, the pallid bat hibernates in sites near its summering grounds, but we have no records of its occurrence during the winter in New Mexico.

Edentates

ORDER EDENTATA

This is an exclusively New World order, and includes anteaters, sloths, and armadillos, as well as the extinct armadillo-like glyptodons. So far as we can tell, edentates evolved in South America during its time of isolation, and in the past few million years a few kinds entered North America. The immigrants from South America included the bear-sized ground sloths, which once lived in New Mexico but have since become extinct. At present, the only edentate which lives in the United States is the nine-banded armadillo, which may occasionally enter our state.

Although the word *edentate* means without teeth, the only truly toothless edentates are the anteaters. Armadillos have a large number of simple peg-like teeth which, unlike the teeth of most other mammals, lack the hard outer covering of enamel. There are many kinds of armadillos in South America, ranging in size from the tiny fairy armadillo, which can readily fit in a human palm, to the giant armadillo, which may weigh more than a hundred pounds.

Nine-Banded Armadillo

Dasypus novencinctus. It is not certain that there are extant populations of armadillos in New Mexico. A few shells have been found in the San Simon Sink of the extreme southeastern part of the state, but they may be of prehistoric origin. Two were observed dead on the highway near Santa Rosa, but the specimens were not preserved. Since the northern limit of the geographic range of the armadillo is seemingly determined by winter low temperatures, it may be that during warm cycles in the past the animals entered our state for brief periods. *Dasypus* is common farther south and east in Texas, and is also found in western Mexico about as far north as Mazatlán.

Armadillos are burrowing animals that feed chiefly upon invertebrates and small vertebrates. Pairs are formed during the breeding season. Reproduction is distinctive because the female almost always produces identical quadruplets from one fertilized egg. The young are born in an advanced stage of development, with their eyes open, and are able to follow the mother on foraging expeditions a few hours after birth. These animals are unusually tolerant to oxygen deprivation, which is a possible adaptation to subterranean life.

Rabbit-Like Mammals

ORDER LAGOMORPHA

This group includes rabbits, hares, and pikas. All of these animals are somewhat rodentlike in their possession of enlarged gnawing front teeth or incisors. Indeed, at one time, all of these kinds were placed in the order Rodentia. However, lagomorphs differ in many ways from rodents, and are probably not very closely related to them.

Although the enlarged incisors of rabbits superficially resemble those of rodents, lagomorphs have two upper incisors on each side, for a total of four, while rodents have a total of two. The incisors of lagomorphs are completely covered with enamel, while those of rodents have enamel on the front surface only. In both orders the front incisors grow throughout life.

Lagomorphs feed entirely on plant material. Like most plant feeders, they have developed specializations to enable them to maximize the benefit they receive from eating material low in nutrient value and sometimes difficult to digest. In particular, lagomorphs have developed reingestion, a phenomenon whereby certain fecal pellets still containing valuable nutrients are eaten, or reingested, so that even more food value may be extracted from them. An analogous practice among ruminant animals is to bring partially digested food up from the stomach so that it may be chewed again and mixed with salivary enzymes: "chewing the cud."

There are two families of lagomorphs: the rabbits and hares (Leporidae) are distinguished by conspicuous long ears and elongate hind feet and legs. Pikas (Ochotonidae) have short, rounded ears and normally proportioned limbs. Leporids are found almost worldwide and are common in many habitats, while pikas are limited to northern parts of Eurasia and to mountainous regions of western North America.

PIKAS

Family Ochotonidae

The name "pika," probably of Asiatic (Afghanistani) origin, should be pronounced "pee-ka," referring to the piping or whistling calls made by the animals. The name "coney," sometimes applied to these animals, derives from Latin *cuniculus,* a rabbit, and is thus related to Spanish *conejo,* also meaning rabbit.

In the Old World, pikas are widespread in northern parts of Asia, where some live in mountains and others in grasslands. In North America, the animals are strictly associated with rock slides; they may be found as low as sea level in northern regions, but ascend to ever increasing altitudes in more southern regions.

Pika

Ochotona princeps.   Pikas are gray animals the size of guinea pigs, with no visible tail, short legs, and short rounded ears. They are almost always seen in or near rock slides at high elevations in the mountains of northern New Mexico, where they have been recorded from the Jemez and Sangre de Cristo ranges. In the spruce-fir forests or in the alpine zone, you may see a pika if you watch carefully for the animals perched on prominent rocks in the talus slopes. They may also be detected by listening for their distinctive voice: a short nasal call, somewhat like a very abbreviated bleat of a sheep or goat.

During the summer, pikas are busy gathering and curing hay for winter use. They may cut large quantities of vegetation, which they spread out in exposed sites for curing in the sun. These hay piles are then stored for later use. Each pika maintains a territory that is centered upon the hay pile. Territories of males and females overlap, but within each sex the territories are mutually exclusive. Young animals may have their own territories in less favorable habitats. The ownership of territories is advertised by calling and by scent-marking. Among the territory holders, a dominance hierarchy exists which is based upon age, size, and sex. Males are generally dominant to females, and older animals dominate juveniles. Choice territories are those with plenty of pasture and ready access to extensive shelter.

Pikas are diurnal, and are active all year. At night, they produce a distinctive kind of fecal pellet, which is black and wrapped in a gelatinous substance. The pikas eat the nighttime droppings, which then may yield additional nutrients.

Mating takes place in summer, and after a gestation period of about thirty days, from two to six young are born. Females may be receptive to mating immediately after they give birth, and thus there exists the possibility of producing more than one litter a year.

Pikas are subject to attack by a variety of predators, and among these, the members of the weasel family may be quite important. *Ochotona* is of no economic significance to man, but these attractive little animals are certainly an important component of the lure of the high country for many people.

RABBITS AND HARES

Family Leporidae

Members of this family are readily recognized by their extremely long ears, long hind legs, and very short tail. All are herbivorous, foraging mostly during the hours of twilight or darkness, though some may be observed feeding in late afternoon or as late as nine o'clock in the morning.

New Mexican leporids are correctly referred to as hares (genus *Lepus*) or as rabbits (genus *Sylvilagus*). Hares are larger and differ from rabbits because they do not construct a nest and their young are born in a well-developed condition with their eyes open and their bodies fully furred (precocial). Young hares are able to hop and follow the parent within a few days of birth. Hares tend to avoid predators by running away. Rabbits construct a shallow nest, which the female lines with fur plucked from her underside. The young are born naked and blind (altricial), and can leave the nest only after a period of growth and development. Rabbits flee from predators, but usually seek shelter quickly in a burrow or in dense cover. *Lepus californicus* and *L. townsendii* are usually referred to as jackrabbits, and *L. americanus* is sometimes called the snowshoe rabbit. Nonetheless, all three are correctly called hares. Members of the genus *Sylvilagus* are usually called cottontails, or cottontail rabbits. When a cottontail runs away from you, its fluffy white tail is very conspicuous, serving to identify it as a rabbit rather than as a hare. Some hares have all-white tails—for example, the white-tailed jackrabbit (*L. townsendii*), but all our hares have distinctively black-tipped ears that cottontails lack. The skulls of rabbits differ from those of hares in certain technical features. For example, in *Sylvilagus* the interparietal bone forms a distinct entity in adults, while that of members of the genus *Lepus* is fused to the parietal bones.

HARES

Genus *Lepus*

Four species occur in New Mexico. The snowshoe hare (*L. americanus*) is limited in its distribution to the higher parts of the San Juan and Sangre de Cristo ranges, where it occurs in forested areas. It might be confused with the mountain cottontail (*Sylvilagus nuttalli*), which occurs in the same places; but the hare has black ear tips, usually has white feet in summer, and turns white in winter. The white-tailed jackrabbit (*L. townsendii*) is found in the same general part of the state, but it inhabits open areas rather than forests, has an all white tail, and is gray (rather than brown) in summer. The black-tail jack (*L. californicus*) is the most common species in the state, and is recognizable by the huge black-tipped ears, black top to the tail, and because it is usually seen in open desert and grassland areas. The white-sided jack (*L. callotis*) is found only in southern Hidalgo County. It combines a black-topped tail and large ears that lack black tips.

Snowshoe Hare

Lepus americanus. Snowshoe hares occupy the spruce-fir forest zone of the Sangre de Cristo and San Juan mountains in New Mexico. They have been reported in the Jemez Mountains, but because no specimens have been taken their occurrence awaits confirmation.

Within their geographic range in the state, snowshoe hares prefer forests with a dense understory of shrubs and small trees. They do not construct burrows or nests, but rest by day in depressions in thick cover. The diet consists of various vegetative parts of plants, including the bark and cambial layers of small trees. Some reports suggest that carrion may occasionally be consumed.

Each female hare has a territory of several acres from which other females are excluded. Males appear to have a territory that includes those of several females with which they consort. One or two litters of four or five young are born each year. As with all hares, the young are precocial, but tend to spend their early days hidden together in deep cover.

Populations of snowshoe hares vary in size from year to year, and appear to go from high to low over an approximately nine-year cycle. When numbers increase and the hare population grows quite dense, the animals are known to succumb to "shock disease," possibly adreno-pituitary exhaustion resulting from the severe stress of the crowded conditions. In Canada, where these cycles have been studied for many years, the populations of carnivores which depend upon the hares, such as the lynx, are also cyclic. This cyclic behavior has not been recorded in New Mexico.

In fall, the shortening daylength so affects the hares that their hair follicles produce white rather than brown hairs. When the animals moult during this season, they gradually turn white and are thus pro-tectively colored against a background of snow. In late winter this trend is reversed. The hind feet of these hares have an especially broad web of hairs during the winter, and this facilitates walking and running over the deep snow. Snowshoe hares are difficult to find in summer or in winter, but in winter their characteristic tracks are easily recognized.

White-Tailed Jack

Lepus townsendii.   White-tailed jacks are common in the northern plains and grasslands, but barely enter New Mexico. During glacial times, this species occurred as far south as Eddy County. Our few records from the state are from the sage plains of the Rio Grande Valley near Taos, and from the high grasslands of the San Juan Mountains. In those areas where white- and black-tailed jacks occur together, the white-tails prefer open grasslands, while black-tails select shrublands. In more northern areas, white-tails molt to a whitish pelage in the winter, but it is not known if this is true in New Mexico.

Black-Tailed Jack

Lepus californicus.   This is, by far, the most common jackrabbit in New Mexico. In any part of the state except the high northern moun-tains, a jackrabbit that you see is almost certain to belong to this spe-cies. Black-tailed jacks may enter open ponderosa pine forest, but, in general, they are most common in more open treeless habitats. They seem to prefer deserts and grasslands with a sparse cover of shrubs, beneath which they may shelter from the sun and from predators. Overgrazing, resulting in an increase in shrubs, enhances the habitat for jackrabbits; and it may further contribute to the deterioration of rangeland because the hares tend to graze forage more severely than cattle. Jackrabbits tend to congregate in areas where there is green forage, such as alfalfa or wheat fields; and some old reports suggest that they may also collect in places where local rains have caused the native vegetation to green up. Possibly, the ability to cover large areas at little cost may be part of the usual foraging strategy of the animals.

Little is known of the social habits of this species. Courtship involves prolonged chases of the female by the male. Ovulation is induced by copulation, as in most leporids. After from forty-one to forty-seven days, one to eight young are born. As in all *Lepus,* the young are born fully furred and with their eyes open, and they are able to follow the mother soon after birth. By ten days of age the young begin taking solid food, and after ten weeks of growth they have attained 90 percent of adult size.

Many carnivorous animals prey upon jackrabbits, although the adults are probably hard to capture for most predators. The usual method of escape is by fleeing at high speed, up to forty miles per hour. These animals lack stamina, however, and may be run down by persistent pursuit. Coyotes reportedly may take advantage of this weakness by pursuing them in relays.

Jackrabbits host a variety of diseases. Some of them, such as tularemia and bubonic plague, may be transmitted to humans. Although the animals are good eating, it is wise to avoid individuals which behave lethargically. Despite their deleterious effects on rangeland, jackrabbits are such an important food for such carnivores as coyotes and bobcats that the hares may act as a buffer between the predators and domestic livestock. Predator-control programs sometimes seem to release jackrabbits from the depressing effects of predation, resulting in increases in their numbers and thus adding pressure on the rangeland. Studies in southern Arizona indicate that approximately thirty jackrabbits equal one sheep in food consumed, while one hundred forty-eight are equivalent to one cow.

White-Sided Jack

Lepus callotis.   For many years it was not certain that this species of the Mexican Plateau lived in New Mexico. Then, in 1974, a number of individuals were seen and identified in the vicinity of the old Cloverdale store in the southern Animas Valley of Hidalgo County. Since that time the species has been recorded in that area fairly regularly, and seems to inhabit stands of tabosa grass (*Hilaria mutica*), while the much more common black-tailed jack is found in more overgrazed areas with a cover of sparse shrubs.

RABBITS

Genus *Sylvilagus*

Three species of Sylvilagus occur in New Mexico: the eastern cottontail (*S. floridanus*), the mountain cottontail (*S. nuttalli*), and the desert cottontail (*S. auduboni*). The three kinds are so similar that careful examination of preserved specimens, especially the cleaned skulls, is essential for correct identification. Even experts have difficulty in distinguishing them in the field. The first two species are chiefly inhabitants of montaine forests, usually from the ponderosa pine forests upward. These mountain animals are relatively uncommon and seldom seen. Desert cottontails are found from the piñon-juniper woodland down through desert and grassland habitats. They are widespread and abundant in New Mexico, and most cottontails you see in all likelihood, belong to this species. The desert cottontail is smaller, more slender, and has longer ears, with enlarged tympanic bullae: those capsules of bone on the skull which house the middle-ear bones and, by being larger, enhance the rabbit's ability to hear well in dry air. The two montane species are heavier-bodied and have shorter appendages. The mountain cottontail has been recorded from the Jemez, San Juan, Sangre de Cristo, and Chuska mountains, while the eastern cottontail occupies those mountains further to the south.

Cottontails inhabit places where they may retreat to cover when danger threatens. Sometimes the cover is thick brush, rocks, or the burrow of a skunk, badger, or other burrowing animal. Most feeding is done at dawn or dusk, or during the night. They consume a variety of plant materials, including leaves, stems, flowers, roots, and bark. Much of the water needed by the animals probably comes from their food.

Rabbits do not seem to be territorial, but the males behave aggressively toward one another during the mating season. Each rabbit occupies a home range, which may be several acres in extent. Some evidence suggests that the home ranges of males may be larger than those of females. Males court females by chasing them and sometimes by urinating on them. After twenty-five to thirty-five days, the female produces a litter of two to six blind and naked young. Desert cottontails may have slightly fewer young than eastern or mountain species, and there is some evidence that animals living at higher elevations or latitudes may have more young than those from the lowlands or more southern places. This trend has not been confirmed for New Mexico. Three or four litters a year are produced per female, again probably depending on the length of the growing season. The eyes of the young open at four or five days of age, and after fourteen or fifteen days the youngsters can leave the nest. Females may mate soon after bearing their young. In cottontails, as with hares, the male probably plays no part in the rearing of the young.

Cottontails are preyed upon by many kinds of avian, mammalian, and reptilian carnivores. We once took a full-grown desert cottontail from the stomach of a large western diamondback rattler in the Sandía foothills. Since prehistoric times in New Mexico, cottontails have been good food for humans. Thousands of rabbit bones have been recovered from archaeological sites in the state. As with other leporids, the human rabbit hunter should beware of sluggish or emaciated cottontails, which may harbor transmittable diseases.

Rodents

ORDER RODENTIA

Most mammals are rodents, both from the standpoint of number of kinds and of individuals. A recent estimate indicates that of the approximately 4,100 kinds of mammals known to exist, about 1,700 are rodents. Seventy-five kinds of rodents are known to inhabit New Mexico.

Rodents are characterized by the possession of two upper and two lower gnawing front teeth or incisors. These teeth are covered with enamel on the front surface only, with the rest of the tooth being made of dentine. The teeth are continually growing. As they grow, the rodent wears them away by gnawing on hard substances. Because the backs wear more rapidly than the front, the tooth is self-sharpening, much like a chisel that is made of harder metal on the front than on the back. Behind the incisors is a toothless gap, the diastema, into which fur-covered folds of the lips protrude from the sides, so that when the incisors are in use they are essentially outside of the mouth, and spoil from the gnawing operation doesn't enter unless the rodent wishes. Behind the diastema are the cheek teeth of rodents, consisting of molars and sometimes premolars, which vary in structure and number depending upon their function. Rodents are preeminent vegetarians, feeding on all parts of plants. There are specialists in roots, bark, leaves, seeds, and other sorts of fruit, while other kinds eat insects, meat, eggs, and fish. All sorts of locomotor patterns are practiced by rodents. Jumpers, runners, swimmers, climbers, burrowers, and gliders are well known. Some kind of rodent is found almost everywhere in the world, except for Antarctica.

Because there are so many rodents, it is important for anyone who wants to study them to first learn some of the major categories. Most rodents in New Mexico are squirrels (family Sciuridae, twenty species), pocket gophers (family Geomyidae, five species), kangaroo rats or pocket mice (family Heteromyidae, ten species), native mice or rats (family Cricetidae, twenty-four species), or voles (family Arvicolidae, eight species). In addition there is also one beaver, one porcupine, two jumping mice (family Zapodidae), three non-native mice and rats (family Muridae), and the introduced nutria (family Capromyidae). Beavers are very large aquatic rodents with dorsoventrally flattened and scaly tails. Porcupines are very large rodents covered with long black and yellow quills. Jumping mice are small, with very long tails and long hind feet. They could be confused with kangaroo rats, but the latter have external fur-lined cheek pouches, long hairs on the tips of their tails, and are found in dry desert and grassland, while jumping mice are usually found in the mountains, near water or in marshy areas along the Rio Grande. The nutria is a medium-sized brown aquatic rodent, with a long *round* scaly tail and four webbed hindtoes. The non-native rats and mice have a nearly hairless, long scaly tail, and tend *not to be sharply bicolored* in pattern. That leaves the four big families. All of our squirrels are out in the daytime (diurnal) and have well-haired, sometimes bushy tails. The tails may be long or short, and the squirrel may live in almost any kind of habitat—not necessarily in a tree! Pocket gophers have short hairless tails, very small eyes, large front claws, and external fur-lined cheek pouches. Except for brief excursions on the surface, they live underground and throw up large mounds of dirt; and in places where there is snow much of the winter, they fill snow tunnels with dirt to make long, ropy dirt cores that festoon mountain meadows when the snow melts. Pocket mice and kangaroo rats also have external fur-lined cheek pouches, but unlike gophers, they *have* elongate tails and *don't have* elongate front claws. Everything else is a member of the family Cricetidae or Arvicolidae.

SQUIRRELS

Family Sciuridae

New Mexican squirrels fall into three categories: tree squirrels (genera *Sciurus* and *Tamiasciurus*), ground squirrels (genera *Spermophilus*,

Ammospermophilus, Marmota, and *Cynomys*), and chipmunks (genus *Eu-tamias*). Tree squirrels forage and nest in trees, and have large bushy tails. Ground squirrels live in burrows in the ground, or under or among rocks. One kind, the rock squirrel (*Spermophilus variegatus*), has a bushy gray tail and is sometimes seen in trees, but it seeks shelter underground when pursued. Chipmunks may be seen on the ground or in trees, and usually they nest on or near the ground, under a log or rock and sometimes in a burrow. Chipmunks are characterized by a pattern of two lateral white stripes bordered by black, a middorsal black stripe, and a set of facial stripes. The golden-mantled ground squirrel (*Spermophilus lateralis*) and the antelope ground squirrel (*Ammospermophilus*) have white lateral stripes. A fourth group of squirrels, the flying squirrels (genus *Glaucomys*), consists of nocturnal gliding species, but it is not represented in New Mexico.

TREE SQUIRRELS

Sciurus and *Tamiasciurus*

The two common tree squirrels in New Mexico are the tassle-eared or Abert squirrel (*Sciurus aberti*) and the chickaree, red, or spruce squirrel (*Tamiasciurus hudsonicus*). The chickaree is found in mixed coniferous and in spruce-fir forests in the higher mountains. It is reddish above, white below, with a black lateral stripe separating the two colors. Tassle-ears are larger, inhabit ponderosa forests, are gray above and white below, and have a tail that is white ventrally. Most strikingly, each ear is provided with a long conspicuous tuft of hair. There is some overlap in habitat between the two tree squirrels: chickarees may be found in the ponderosa zone, and tassle-ears in the mixed coniferous, but ordinarily the habitat difference is fairly well observed. In some places where tassle-ears have been introduced, there is evidence that they have succeeded at the expense of the chickaree.

Two other kinds of tree squirrels within our borders are rare and local in distribution. The Arizona gray squirrel (*Sciurus arizonensis*) is all gray dorsally and white ventrally, lacks ear tufts, and is found only in the lower riparian forests of the San Francisco River drainage in Catron County. The fox squirrel (*S. niger*) is grayish black above and orangish-yellow ventrally. It has been recorded only in Roswell, where it may have been introduced.

Chickaree

Tamiasciurus hudsonicus. These small squirrels are resident in those mountains in the state which are high enough to support stands of spruce. In the extensive spruce forests of the Jemez and Sangre de Cristo mountains, chickarees are widespread and common. In the smaller southern mountain ranges, where the stands of spruce may be limited in extent to moist north-facing areas, the squirrels are rare and local. Although these animals are known to eat a diversity of plant foods, and also to eat the occasional bird, egg, or insect, they seem to specialize in the cones of certain conifers in our region, especially Englemann and blue spruce, and Douglas fir. When spruce cones are ripening in summer the squirrels are busy with their harvest, and they may be located easily by the attentive naturalist who listens for the sound of cones falling to the forest floor as the squirrel cuts and drops them one by one. After a session of cutting, the squirrel gathers the cones from the ground and buries them in a pile of old cone scales left over from the feeding activities of the previous year. The cones may also be secreted in crevices of dead trees and in other places, but a requirement of the cache site is that it be cool and damp so that the cones will not dry out and open. When they are needed the cones are excavated, torn apart, and the seeds eaten. The resulting pile of scales may become very large over a period of a year or two, and is called a kitchen midden. These middens, usually one or two per squirrel, serve to mark the squirrels' territory and allow the observer to estimate the number of animals in the woods. Each squirrel tends to defend its patch of trees centered about a midden. Cones of Douglas fir are also stored, but fir (*Abies*) cones are seldom found in red squirrel middens because the cone scales fall while the cones are still upright on the trees, allowing the winged seeds to disperse before the squirrels can harvest the whole packet. The squirrels are active all winter long, often tunneling through the snow to reach their buried caches.

During the breeding season, male squirrels enter the territory of an estrous female who is receptive for one day per estrus. After a gestation of thirty-five to thirty-eight days, the blind and hairless young are born in a hollow cavity of an outside nest fashioned of plant material and constructed on a branch near the trunk. The eyes of the young open and the body is fully furred by about twenty-eight days, when the adolescents may begin to leave the nest. Probably, in most of New Mexico, a single litter is produced each year.

Red squirrels are sometimes hunted for food, but their flesh tends to be flavored by the coniferous plants on which they feed, and it is not very palatable to most people.

Tassle-Eared Squirrel

Sciurus aberti.   Abert squirrels are widespread, but rarely very abundant, in the ponderosa pine forests of New Mexico. The squirrels shelter in the pines and rely heavily upon them for food. There is some evidence that, in turn, the pines have taken steps to defend themselves against the squirrels. The squirrels eat pine seeds, buds, and the cambial layers under the bark of small twigs. When the squirrels are feeding on a tree, they cut sections of twig four or five inches long, peel off the bark, and consume the cambium. The clumps of needles dropped during this operation and the peeled sections of twig serve to identify a site where the squirrels have been feeding. After some practice, it is possible to recognize squirrel-feeding trees from a distance because of their thinner appearance. It appears that the squirrels select certain trees and leave others alone. Laboratory tests suggest that captive squirrels prefer products from the same trees that wild ones select, and refuse food from trees that are refused by the free animals. Seemingly, many trees, but not all, have succeeded in elaborating chemical defenses against Abert squirrel predation. Some populations of squirrels may have succeeded in overcoming these defenses, but this has not been demonstrated.

During the breeding season, several males pursue estrous females. Among these males, one seems to be dominant and obtains most of the copulations, but the other males may succeed in copulating with the female as well. After a gestation of about forty days, two to four blind and naked young are born in a nest constructed on the branches of a ponderosa or some other kind of tree. The babies reach adult size at fifteen to sixteen weeks of age. One or two litters a year are produced by each female. Home ranges of the adults extend from ten to twenty acres.

Abert squirrels are hunted for food, but they are seldom common enough to make squirrel hunting an important sport in New Mexico.

Arizona Gray Squirrel

Sciurus arizonensis.   This species is widespread in the valleys transecting the Mogollon Plateau of Arizona, and is found on some isolated mountains of southern Arizona; but in our state it appears to be confined to the montane valleys in western Catron County. There, its principal habitat seems to be riparian woodlands of walnuts, sycamores, and cottonwoods. Probably, walnuts are important for its occurrence; individuals have been seen whose face and underparts were so stained with the brown juice from walnut husks that the identity of the animals was at first uncertain. This squirrel sometimes occurs at higher elevations. A party from Tulane University found one at Willow Creek, in the mixed coniferous forest of the Mogollon Mountains. Little information seems to be available concerning the Arizona gray squirrel.

Fox Squirrel

Sciurus niger.   The fox squirrel is abundant over much of the central and eastern United States, but its natural range may not include New Mexico. These animals are common in Roswell, but have not been detected elsewhere in the state. In the Great Plains, the fox squirrel extends westward along those river valleys that have riparian woodlands. In this way, the species has reached the Rocky Mountains along the North Platte, and occur in the Denver–Fort Collins area probably as a result of introductions. The nearest place where native fox squirrels occur along the Pecos River is close to its confluence with the Rio Grande in Terrel County, Texas. Suitable forested habitat does not exist along the Pecos between this area and Roswell, and it thus seems unlikely that the animals have made it into New Mexico on their own. The Roswell population probably originated from intentional introductions, but there seems to be no firm information on this point.

CHIPMUNKS

Eutamias

Chipmunks are found in most wooded and forested areas of New Mexico. They are common in montane forests, but, especially in the northern and western part of the state, may be common in piñon-juniper woodland as well. These small squirrels are active during the day, foraging for a variety of plant food, chiefly flowers, seeds, and other reproductive parts gathered mostly on or near the ground. They are good climbers, however, and may be seen high in forest trees. As feeders they are generalists; that is, they gather foods as they come into season, or as the animals encounter small patches of fruiting or flowering vegetation. Chipmunk food becomes most common from mid- to late summer and autumn, when the animals are busy much of the day in hoarding food for the winter season. Since chipmunks store very little fat, they are dependent upon their caches of food to take them through a long winter. During the winter the animals may become torpid in their burrows, arousing only at intervals to feed on their stores. Hibernating ground squirrels, on the other hand, subsist through their winter period of torpidity on their stored body fat. Because the late summer period of food-gathering is so critical to their winter survival, they are very aggressive in situations where more than one animal locates a patch of good food. Nonetheless, chipmunks are not territorial in the classical sense of defending an area, although each individual has a home range of two to four acres within which it seeks food and shelter.

Copulation takes place shortly after the animals emerge from hibernation in late February or March. Some evidence suggests that males may emerge slightly before females. After a gestation period of thirty to thirty-three days, the females bear a litter of four to six blind and hairless young. The young remain in the nest for about five weeks, and are weaned and independent of the female at six to seven weeks of age. By mid-April the testes of adult males have regressed in size and retreated to the abdominal cavity. After the young are weaned, the female molts and does not become sexually active again until the next year. Thus, one litter per season per female is the general rule. Young animals are sexually mature in about a year. Those who have kept chipmunks as captives note that even if born and raised in captivity they never become accustomed to the presence of humans. Nonetheless, wild chipmunks often learn to approach humans and accept food from their hands.

Five species of chipmunk are to be found in New Mexico. All are rather similar and may be difficult to identify, especially in the field. Most distinctive is the cliff chipmunk, *Eutamias dorsalis*. This species is characterized by a gray wash over the dorsal surface that tends to obscure the stripes. *E. dorsalis* is found only west of the Rio Grande, and mostly in the mountains south of Interstate-40, though they have been taken in the Chuskas and at Mount Taylor. The remaining four species are divided into least chipmunks (*E. minimus*) and forest chipmunks (*E. quadrivittatus, E. cinereicollis,* and *E. canipes*). Least chipmunks are the smallest. The hind feet measure 32 millimeters or less; the upper lip is buffy (rather than whitish); and the lateral dark stripes are black rather than brownish. Forest chipmunks are larger, have whitish or grayish upper lips, and the lateral stripes are frequently brownish. Unfortunately, all of these characteristics are variable enough so that specimens occur which cannot be definitely identified without detailed study of the skull and of the penis bone or baculum. In any event, these traits are all but impossible to use for field identification. Geography is quite helpful in field identification. *Eutamias canipes* is found only in the Gallinas, Sacramento, Sierra Blanca, and Guadalupe ranges. It is the only chipmunk in these mountains except that the least chipmunk occurs high on

Sierra Blanca and in James Canyon on the east side of the Sacramentos. In both places the least chipmunk is very rare; most chipmunks seen in that area are probably *canipes*. In the hand, *canipes* may be told from the other forest chipmunks by the dorsal surfaces of its hind feet, which are *gray* rather than tan or brownish. *Eutamias cinereicollis* is found only west of the Rio Grande and south of Interstate-40, in the mountains of Socorro, Catron, Sierra, and Grant counties. There, it may coexist with the cliff chipmunk. If both occur on the same mountain, the cliff chipmunk is usually lower, in piñon-juniper woodland or ponderosa forest, while *cinereicollis* is in the mixed coniferous or spruce-fir forest. In Beartrap Canyon, in the northern San Mateo Mountains, *dorsalis* is found in the woodland and ponderosa forest on the drier slopes, while *cinereicollis* is found among the spruces and firs on the moist shaded slopes and in the canyon bottom, where some ground water makes for mesic condition. In the hand, *cinereicollis* may be told from other forest chipmunks by the brownish dorsal surface of the hind feet, and the grayish collar around the back of the neck. *Eutamias quadrivittatus* is found from the Manzanos, Zuñis, and Mount Taylor northward. An isolated colony also occupies the Organ Mountains. It is not confined to forests, and may occur in rich piñon-juniper woodland as well. In most of the northern mountains this species is found together with the least chipmunk. Where the two occur together there is usually some habitat separation. *Eutamias quadrivittatus* is most common in piñon, juniper, and oak woodland and in ponderosa and mixed coniferous forest, while *minimus* is common in spruce-fir forest or below the range of *quadrivittatus* in sage grasslands. In California, it has been shown that the least chipmunk tends to be subordinate to forest chipmunks in aggressive encounters, and that it has an increased tolerance of dry, arid conditions. Whether this is true in our area is not known.

Yellow-Bellied Marmot

Marmota flaviventris.   Marmots are very large, the size of a house cat or larger. They have a short bushy tail and tend to be yellowish brown, and grayish or blackish in overall coloration. They are most often seen sunning themselves on rocks or foraging in meadows at high elevations in the Sangre de Cristo Mountains. There, they occur in meadows in the spruce-fir forest, and in rock slides from about eleven thousand feet up to well above timberline. They have also been recorded in the San Juan Mountains in the Chama and Canjilon regions. During the waning phases of the last glacial age in New Mexico, approximately ten thousand years ago, marmots were found as far south as Eddy and Catron counties.

Marmots live as single individuals, as pairs, or in harems consisting of a territorial male and several females and their young. Soon after emergence from hibernation, mating takes place. After a gestation period of approximately thirty days, four to five young are born. Young remain in the burrow for twenty to thirty days, after which they are weaned. Only one litter per year is produced. Females may not breed for the first two or three years of life. Because of the short growing season at the high altitudes where marmots live, the young must hurry to accumulate enough body fat to allow them to survive a hibernation period of eight months. Hibernation is probably the period of greatest mortality for young and adults alike. Marmots do suffer some predation from coyotes, badgers, eagles, and, of course, humans.

PRAIRIE DOGS

Cynomys

Prairie dogs are medium-sized tan squirrels with very short tails. They are most often seen sitting upright near a burrow in open grassy areas, frequently near highways. No other New Mexican ground squirrel is this large, and no other has a short *black-tipped* or *white-tipped* tail. Other ground squirrels, which have a generally similar appearance, are smaller and have a pattern of stripes or spots dorsally. Two species are found in our state. The blacktail prairie dog, *Cynomys ludovicianus*, has a black-tipped tail, occurs in large colonies, and occupies grasslands in the eastern half of the state. The Gunnison prairie dog, *C. gunnisoni*, has a white-tipped tail, occurs in small groups, and is found in the northwestern third of the state.

Both species are highly social, but the blacktail probably has the most elaborate social structure of any American rodent. The animals formerly occurred in huge towns, which in the early days stretched for miles over the western Great Plains and contained millions of individuals. The colonies are broken into smaller subdivisions by topographic markers such as hills or arroyos. These smaller units, known as wards, are subdivided on social grounds into coteries. The coterie consists of a male and several females and their young. Members of the coterie defend the area against outsiders, but are congenial among themselves. The coterie boundaries are advertised by a variety of vocal and postural signals. Coterie members may greet each other by kissing: opening the mouth and touching each other's incisors. Each animal occupies a burrow, the entrance of which is in the center of a doughnut-shaped mound that serves to prevent water from entering. Often inside the entrance is a turnaround chamber. The animals become fat in the fall and spend much of the winter underground. However, there are records of aboveground activity for every month of the year. Although the animals become torpid in winter, they may emerge from time to time. After spring emergence, mating takes place. Approximately four young are born after a gestation period of about thirty days. The young emerge in about thirty days, but remain in the vicinity of the home burrow for some additional time. Young males tend to leave the coterie and set up homes in new areas, while young females remain in the natal neighborhood. The young are capable of reproduction in a year, but many females may wait until their second year to bear young of their own.

Gunnison prairie dogs occur in much smaller colonies, perhaps so few as three or four individuals, and do not have the elaborate system of the blacktails. The burrow entrances of *gunnisoni* have a mound of earth at the side, rather than surrounding the hole as in the burrows of blacktails.

Both species of prairie dogs are preyed upon by hawks and eagles, as well as by mammalian carnivores such as badgers and weasels. The most famous predator is the black-footed ferret (*Mustela nigripes*), which has become nearly extinct as a result of the tremendous reduction in numbers of prairie dogs. Because *Cynomys* feeds upon grass as well as a variety of annual weeds, they are competitors for food with domestic livestock. As a result, humans have devoted a great deal of effort to eliminating the "dogs" from rangeland, chiefly by poisoning. In 1908, Vernon Bailey, working for the U.S. Biological Survey, traveled from Deming to Hachita and through the Animas and Playas valleys in what is now southern Hidalgo County. He reported that the area was one continuous prairie dog town, and estimated that the county contained 6,400,000 animals. In numerous trips through exactly the same region during the period from 1955 thru 1972, workers from the Museum of Southwestern Biology never saw a single prairie dog! Similar devastation has visited the animals in many parts of their former range. In this respect, blacktails have suffered more than Gunnisons. The latter species may be seen more or less regularly in various parts of northwestern New Mexico. Both species are subject to bubonic plague, and are periodically decimated by the disease.

ANTELOPE GROUND SQUIRRELS

Ammospermophilus

These dark-backed ground squirrels have a white lateral stripe running from the shoulder to the hip on either side. The bushy tail is carried well over the animal's back. Antelope squirrels inhabit shrub desert or rocky foothill terrain, and may be found in the lower juniper zone, but usually not much higher. Unlike other ground squirrels, prairie dogs, and chipmunks, *Ammospermophilus* is active throughout the year. Even during the hottest summer weather, they may be seen foraging above ground. During these foraging bouts the squirrels may overheat slightly, then retire to the cooler temperatures of their burrows to cool off. They do not cool evaporatively, and hence are not water-stressed by this behavior. During the summer the squirrels occupy burrows individually, except for the association of females and unweaned young. In the winter, however, the animals live several in a burrow, conserving heat during the night by huddling. They are not territorial, but a linear dominance hierarchy occurs among members of local groups. Four or five young are born in spring after a gestation of about twenty-nine days. The young remain in the burrow for another month before emerging. Females seemingly produce but one litter a year. Since hibernation is not a part of the life history of this species, the young are not under the pressure to accumulate winter reserves that many other squirrels face. Antelope squirrels are omnivores, and in addition to vegetation, they include animal matter in their diets on a regular basis.

Three species of *Ammospermophilus* are found in New Mexico. Slight color differences separate the three, but since each occupies a different part of the state, and since no two kinds have been found in the same area, identification is not a problem. The white-tailed antelope squirrel, *A. leucurus,* is found west of the Rio Grande and as far south as the Socorro area. The white bottom of the tail of this species is quite conspicuous as the animal runs about, and is responsible for its common name, since the pronghorn antelope (*Antilocapra*) also displays a white posterior as it flees. The Texas antelope squirrel, *A. interpres,* is found only east of the Rio Grande from the Guadalupe Mountains north to the Sandías. The ventral surface of the tail of this animal is gray rather than white. The Harris antelope squirrel, *A. harrisi,* is found only in the desert foothills and valleys of western Grant and Hidalgo counties. It also has a gray tail, and is quite difficult to tell from *interpres*. Despite intensive searches by mammalogists, no two of these species have ever been found in contact. Nonetheless, one can stand in the western foothills of the Sandías, where *interpres* occurs, and look westward across the Rio Grande to the rocky areas near the mouth of the Jemez Creek, where a colony of *leucurus* has been located.

SPERMOPHILES

Spermophilus

Five species in this genus occur in New Mexico, but they are so diverse in appearance and habits that it is difficult to generalize about them. The rock squirrel, *S. vareigatus,* is the largest and most arboreal. It is gray with a long bushy tail. The mantled ground squirrel, *S. lateralis,* has a dorsal pattern of two white stripes bordered with black, but unlike the chipmunks, lacks a mid-dorsal black stripe and has no facial striping. The abundant spotted ground squirrel, *S. spilosoma,* is reddish, tan, or grayish with an irregular pattern of small white spots. The thirteen-lined ground squirrel, *S. tridecemlineatus,* has a dorsal pattern of stripes alternating with rows of spots. The Mexican ground squirrel, *S. mexicanus,* possesses rows of spots, but no stripes.

Rock Squirrel

Spermophilus variegatus.   These large gray bushy-tailed squirrels might be confused with the Arizona gray squirrel, *Sciurus arizonensis;* but in that species the gray of the back is solid, not flecked with whitish and blackish colors, and the gray squirrel is limited to a small area in western Grant and Catron counties. Tassle-eared squirrels, *S. aberti,* are also gray and bushy tailed, but they have white or black underparts, long tufts of hair on their ears, a lateral black line separating dorsal from ventral coloration, and often a rusty wash down the middle of the back. Rock squirrels tend to be found in the lower life zones, from about the ponderosa forest down into the desert. They seem to require broken, usually rocky terrain, and are common in rocky hillsides and along arroyos. They are found almost throughout the state, and are absent only from the eastern plains.

The animals may live alone or be arranged in loose colonies. Each individual has a home range, but these may overlap broadly, and territoriality has not been observed. There is some evidence that males may live in groups apart from females. The young may be brought forth from April through the summer. It may be that females can produce two litters a year, but that is not certain. The animals deposit fat in late summer, and many disappear with the advent of cooler weather. However, they may be seen at any time during the winter in more southern areas. Probably the majority hibernate, but this aspect of their biology has received little attention. Rock squirrels are quite vocal, and make a loud, somewhat whistlelike cry, which is a distinctive sound in many New Mexican canyons.

Mantled Ground Squirrel

Spermophilus lateralis.   If you camp or picnic in the northern mountains you are likely to find these beautiful ground squirrels common and relatively tame, easily lured into your campground to gather morsels of food. Many people confuse them with chipmunks because the ground squirrels are striped in a somewhat similar way. However, chipmunks have *prominent facial stripes* which the *Spermophilus* lacks; and chipmunks have a *black stripe right down the middle of the back*, also lacking in the ground squirrels. The ground squirrels do have a white stripe bordered with black or brown on each side of the back.

Mantled ground squirrels are most plentiful in the forested northern mountains, but they are also found in the higher mountains of Grant and Catron counties. They prefer meadows and forest-edge situations where herbaceous vegetation is plentiful. In such places the animals may be quite abundant, dwelling in burrows which they dig in the earth. They are capable of climbing and may be seen in low bushes, but they are much less arboreal than chipmunks. One investigator found that 87 percent of the diet consists of fungi and leaves, with the remainder composed of flowers and fruits as well as some animal matter. In another study, the diet of the mantled squirrel was compared with that of the least chipmunk in an area where both species foraged in the same meadows. The diet of both species was 80 to 90 percent common dandelion (*Taraxacum*). However, the chipmunks concentrated on the flowers and seeds, whereas the ground squirrels ate mostly the stems of the flowers, often cutting off the flower heads before consuming the stems. The abandoned flowers were picked up later by the chipmunks.

In late summer the animals accumulate large quantities of fat, entering hibernation in August or September, with adults beginning to hibernate somewhat earlier than animals of the year that take longer to accumulate the requisite amount of fat. The reproductive organs begin to develop in February, and when the squirrels emerge in March or April they are in breeding condition. After a gestation of twenty-eight days, a litter of two to seven or eight young is born. The females produce but one family per year. Females may defend small areas against other squirrels, but seem unsuccessful in keeping rivals out of any appreciable territory. Among the animals living in the same neighborhood, a dominance hierarchy exists.

Thirteen-Lined Ground Squirrel

Spermophilus tridecemlineatus.   This species occupies higher grasslands, chiefly in the northeastern one-third of the state. Isolated colonies have been detected in the Sacramento–Capitán area, and in the high plains of Socorro and Catron counties. These animals are most abundant in the short-grass regions of the central United States, and are rarely common in New Mexico.

Thirteen-lined squirrels live in loose colonies in areas where the height of the grass is not great. In tall-grass areas, reduction in grass cover results in increases in the abundance of the squirrels. They shelter in burrows which they dig in the earth. Each animal occupies a home range which changes in size with the season. For example, when the males emerge from hibernation they expand their home ranges as they seek mates. The home ranges of females are maximal while they are nursing young. A small area in the center of the home range is frequently defended against other individuals. Mating takes place after the animals emerge in early spring, and four to nine young are born after a gestation of about twenty-eight days. The young are weaned and leave the burrow after about twenty-eight days. Mortality of the young animals is often from 80 to 95 percent. In southern parts of the range of the species two litters per year may be produced. There are no data on this point for New Mexico. Animals may enter hibernation as early as July, and a dormancy of eight months is not unusual. Hibernators arouse periodically. Like many other ground squirrels, this species eats a great deal of animal food. They have been recorded as consuming small vertebrates and a great variety of invertebrates, such as moth larvae and grasshoppers. In some areas a majority of the diet is animal material during some seasons.

Mexican Ground Squirrel

Spermophilus mexicanus.   This is the New Mexican ground squirrel that is most restricted geographically. All the known records for the state are from Eddy, Lea, and Chaves counties. Most are from the Pecos Valley in the vicinity of Roswell, Artesia, and Carlsbad, where they occupy mesquite grassland as well as irrigated farmlands and golf courses.

Evidence on hibernation in this species is equivocal; some naturalists have noted that the animals are active all winter, while others claim that they disappear during cold weather. Mating activity seems to be confined to early spring, March and April. One to ten young are born after a gestation period that has been estimated at thirty days. Details of the development of the young have not been recorded.

Individuals occur in loose colonies. The animals occupy burrows in the earth, defending the burrow and the immediate area against conspecifics. Diet varies seasonally. In spring a preferred food is mesquite, both the beans and the leaves. Later in the year, insects and other small animals make up more than half the menu. These squirrels have been observed eating carrion, and they may be cannibalistic in captivity.

Spotted Ground Squirrel

Spermophilus spilosoma.   This is the most widespread and common of New Mexican ground squirrels, occupying sandy grasslands and desert areas throughout the state. In most such areas in summer, the attentive naturalist may hear the high insectlike trill of this species, even though none may be visible.

These squirrels begin emerging from hibernation in late March. Males generally are active somewhat earlier than females. Mating takes place soon after emergence. The gestation period is not certainly known, but has been estimated at twenty-eight days, and four to twelve young comprise a litter. The young reach adult size in ten to twelve weeks, but the duration of the preweaning period has not been recorded. Pregnant females have been taken as late as August, and it has been suggested that two litters per year may be produced. However, the late pregnancies may be those of one-year-old females, who do not enter sexual receptiveness as early as older individuals. Home range size may reach five to six acres, and is larger for males than for females. Early in the year, spotted squirrels feed heavily on plant food, especially those plants common in sandy and disturbed areas such as tumbleweed, puncturevine, and rice grass. Later in the season, animals become important dietary items.

POCKET GOPHERS

Geomyidae

Although pocket gophers are found throughout New Mexico and may often be active in the daytime, few people have seen them because most of the time these animals live in underground burrows. Gophers are rat-sized rodents with short and mostly hairless tails, extremely short ears, very small eyes, and elongated claws on their forefeet. Close examination of a gopher reveals that on each side of the mouth is a vertical slit leading into a fur-lined pouch of considerable size. The animals are rather sparsely haired and are usually brownish, grayish, or blackish in color. The incisors are large, even by rodent standards, and may be conspicuous in a living animal. In some parts of the country, as in the Midwest, the name "gopher" is applied to a ground squirrel. In the Southeast, pocket gophers are sometimes called "salamanders." In Mexico, the indigenous name *tuza* is sometimes applied; but in other parts of that republic geomyids are referred to by the name *topo*, a derivative of *talpa*, the Latin name for the mole.

Pocket gophers are highly specialized for fossorial (burrowing) life in arid regions. They are thought to have developed these specializations during Miocene time, some 25 million years ago when arid conditions and arid-adapted vegetation developed in the Southwest. Two chief strategies for dealing with aridity have been developed by plants in our region. One strategy involves producing huge numbers of seeds that have the ability to lie dormant for a number of years until conditions are right for germination and growth. When these times arrive, such plants grow in prodigious numbers, producing the vast quantities of seed necessary to ensure that some will survive until the next rainy spell. These plants are exploited by rodents that are seed specialists, such as kangaroo rats and pocket mice, close relatives of the pocket gophers. Other plants have the ability to withstand long periods of drought, and may accomplish this by storing nutrients and water in underground storage parts, such as enlarged roots. These are the plants exploited by pocket gophers. Gophers are able to construct tunnels under the surface of the ground, using their muscular forelegs and enlarged claws, and sometimes their teeth as well. Because vision is of limited use underground, the eyes of gophers are reduced; and because large ears would be an impediment to an animal living in a tight-fitting tunnel, those of pocket gophers are miniscule. As the gopher digs, it kicks the excavated earth behind it with its hind feet. Then, when the loose earth has accumulated, the animal turns, and using its face and forepaws, it pushes the dirt up to the surface of the ground through a temporary entrance to the tunnel. The resulting gopher mounds serve to mark the place where one of the animals is working. After the mound is complete, the gopher seals the entrance, preventing entry by other animals. Gophers consume underground parts of plants, and on occasion they also emerge on the surface to cut and pull green vegetation underground. The animals continue their activity throughout the year. In the mountains, where there is a snow cover, the rodents may emerge on the surface and tunnel through the snow. These snow tunnels are then filled with dirt, and when the snow melts in spring, the ropelike earthern cores are a conspicuous feature of many mountain meadows. Incidently, the cores may retard runoff in such places, thus playing a role in reducing erosion. In irrigated farmlands the gophers' interests may run counter to those of humans. The banks of irrigation ditches are favorite places in which to burrow, and many a farmer has experienced the frustration of having his water run out through a gopher hole, which then enlarges and erodes away the ditch bank. A standard plug for such a hole in some parts of New Mexico is a beer can, which happens to be about the same diameter as a valley pocket gopher. In these agricultural areas, gophers may also be pests because they attack the roots of commercial crops, such as alfalfa. So far as we are aware, the diet of pocket gophers consists almost entirely of vegetation.

Each gopher lives alone in a burrow system which it has constructed. During the breeding season, however, several individuals may be found together in one system. It is believed that the males may enter the burrows of the females to seek copulation. However, there is no permanent pair bond. The burrow system consists of a deeper permanent part and a more superficial set of foraging tunnels. The animal's burrow is simultaneously its home range and territory. In one study, the core of each group of territories was occupied by an adult female. Her system was surrounded by those of younger animals. Adult males seem to construct their burrows so as to be in contact with the greatest possible number of adult females.

Gophers are active throughout the year, but have seasonal cycles in reproduction and burrowing activity. In most species, mating takes place early in the year, with the exact dates depending upon latitude and altitude. Females produce an annual litter of one to seven young after a gestation period of eighteen to twenty-eight days (*Thomomys*). The young disperse in about June, traveling overground to an area adjacent to the burrows of the mother. Predation is especially heavy at this time. By August most young animals have taken up solitary lives. In more southern areas more than one litter a year has been reported, but this information is unavailable for New Mexico. Females may reach sexual maturity during their first year of life, but they may wait until their second year before breeding.

Thomomys, and probably most *Geomys*, breed but once a year, but the limited season of reproduction may be more a function of latitude than of the kind of gopher involved. A southeastern species of *Geomys* breeds throughout the year, and *Pappogeomys*, which has a southern distribution compared to the other two genera, also has a protracted breeding season. One investigator found most of the female *Pappogeomys* that he trapped in the Carlsbad area in February to be in breeding condition. Perhaps because they have less hurried reproductive lives, *Pappogeomys* have fewer young per litter than do *Geomys* or *Thomomys*, an average of 2, rather than 4 to 5 in *Thomomys* or 3 to 4 in *Geomys*. Again, however, the number of young may be related to latitude: the southeastern species of *Geomys* averages from 1.5 to 2 young per litter as does *Pappogeomys*.

The distribution of pocket gophers is strongly influenced by the availability of suitable soils in which the animals may burrow. In New Mexico, and in the West generally, such soils may be patchy in their distribution, with the result that gophers occur in isolated colonies as well. A result of this isolation is that many colonies develop distinctive cranial features, colors, and the like. This marked geographic variation has resulted in the description of many local races or subspecies.

Geomyids are, in general, cantankerous animals, reacting aggressively toward others of their kind or toward individuals of other species of gophers. The result is not only a well-marked territoriality, but a rarity of situations where two kinds coexist on common turf. In a given place only one kind of gopher is generally found, even though, as in part of New Mexico, several species may be available in the region.

Three genera and five species are known within our borders. The genera are readily distinguished by examination of the upper incisors. If the front surfaces of these teeth are smooth with no deep longitudinal grooves, the animal belongs to the genus *Thomomys*. If one groove is present on each tooth, it is a *Pappogeomys*, the chestnut-cheeked gopher, and if two grooves are present on each tooth the creature is a *Geomys*, the plains pocket gopher. The latter two genera have one species each in New Mexico. Both *Geomys* and *Pappogeomys* are found in lowlands in the southeastern one-third of New Mexico. *Thomomys* contains three species which are quite similar, but which tend to be separated geographically. The northern pocket gopher, *T. talpoides*, is found in the Sangre de Cristo, San Juan, Jemez, Chuska, and Mount Taylor ranges. It occurs from about the ponderosa zone upward to the highest available elevations. The Mexican pocket gopher, *T. umbrinus*, is found only in the Animas Mountains, from the foothills upward. All the rest of New Mexico, except for the plains in the eastern one-third of the state, is occupied by the Botta pocket gopher, *T. bottae*. In those places in northern New Mexico where *talpoides* and *bottae* meet on the mountainsides, usually in the ponderosa zone, *talpoides* tends to be gray with large well-marked patches behind its ears. *T. bottae* is brown, with smaller patches. Examination of cleaned skulls may be necessry to identify some individuals.

Two kinds of gopher are rarely found at precisely the same place, but two or more kinds may be found in close proximity and sometimes there are narrow zones of intermingling. In such situations, the different species generally exhibit a tendency to occur in different sorts of habitats. In eastern New Mexico *Geomys bursarius*, *Pappogeomys castanops*, and *Thomomys bottae* may all be found within a few miles of each other. There, *Geomys* is restricted to the deep sandy soils of valleys, while *Pappogeomys* occupies the shallower harder soils of interfluves. *Thomomys* also occupies shallower soils in that region, but seems to be found at slightly higher elevations toward the mountains. *Thomomys* and *Pappogeomys* live quite well in deep sandy soils, but they seem excluded from such places if *Geomys* is present. Where *Thomomys* and *Pappogeomys* occur together, it is often the latter which preempts the deep soils. There is some evidence that the geographic ranges of the pocket gophers have changed recently in the Southwest. *Pappogeomys*, which is now limited to the eastern and southern parts of the state, was found as far north as San Juan County in prehistoric time. Climatic change has been suggested as a factor important in these shifts.

POCKET MICE AND KANGAROO RATS

Family: Heteromyidae

These are perhaps the most distinctive of arid-lands mammals in North America. They are mouse- or rat-sized nocturnal rodents, with medium to very long tails, small ears, and a fur-lined cheek pouch opening on the side of the head just behind the mouth opening, as in pocket gophers. There are three genera of these animals in New Mexico. Kangaroo rats, *Dipodomys*, have enormously elongated hind feet and tails, and they often hop on their hind feet while holding the forefeet tucked close to the chest. These beautiful creatures are tan, brownish, or yellowish on top and white below, with a white stripe, the hip stripe, cutting through the dorsal color above each hind leg. Pocket mice, *Perognathus* and *Chactodipus,* are much smaller than kangaroo rats; have shorter tails and hind feet; lack the hip stripe; and the soles of their hind feet are naked rather than densely covered with fur, as in the kangaroo rats. Pocket mice generally progress by quadrupedal locomotion. Both kinds of animals have the mastoid region of the skull, that portion just above and behind the ear opening, greatly enlarged. Both kinds have highly efficient kidneys, which retain much of the water normally lost in urination. And both kinds have elongate nasal regions on their skulls, which results in the cooling of outgoing air, so that much of the moisture in the exhalation, which normally would be lost, is condensed and retained within the body. Physiologically, the heteromyids are designed so as to minimize water loss. Water conservation is mediated through behavior as well. During the day, the animals remain in underground burrows whose entrances are often sealed. Thus, the humidity remains fairly high, and the cool underground temperature reduces water consumption. A result of these modifications is that heteromyids can, when necessary, subsist on the water contained in the seeds and other vegetation that they eat.

As described in the account of the pocket gophers, heteromyids have specialized on those desert plants which survive aridity by producing huge quantities of seeds that may remain in the soil as a seed bank for years before germination. Pocket mice and kangaroo rats spend much of their above-ground time in searching for these seeds. Since many desert plants produce seeds that blow over the surface of the soil and accumulate in places where the air velocity is less, heteromyids may spend much time in foraging around shrubs and in depressions. However, many seeds are buried as the wind shifts the light desert soils; so the successful seed forager must have the ability to detect buried seeds as well as ones that are lying on the surface. Heteromyids do this by means of their sense of smell. Kangaroo rats, especially, have the ability to detect the odor of underground seeds and to dig them up. Once discovered, the seeds are placed in the cheek pouches and transported to an underground burrow where they may be eaten or stored for future use. Since time spent above ground is time exposed to predators and also to the dry desert air, the prudent heteromyid seeks to minimize that part of the daily activity cycle. This minimization is greatly aided by the ability of the amimal to carry large numbers of seeds per trip, and then to eat in the safety of the burrow. Some studies of radio-tagged kangaroo rats have shown that the animals spend a majority of their time underground.

One of the notable physical and behavioral traits of heteromyids is their tendency to use bipedal locomotion, that is, to hop using the hind legs. This tendency is best developed in kangaroo rats. At first glance, it seems that this locomotor peculiarity must be related to the need for rapid escape from predators. Indeed, when a kangaroo rat is pursued it may resort to a series of wild bipedal leaps, each in a different direction so that the predator cannot predict the direction of the animal's flight. Such locomotion has been called "ricochetal" because the path of the animal resembles that of a randomly bouncing projectile. There is no doubt that such an escape tactic is effective, as the human pursuer of a kangaroo rat can attest. However, it has also been suggested that bipedal locomotion evolved in response to the need for the animals to keep their hands free while foraging, so that seeds could be manipulated into the pouch. While the rat is handling seeds, its dorsally placed eyes make it possible for the animal to keep watch for approaching predators, and because the center of gravity of the creature is over the elongate hind feet, it can essentially hop forward, keeping the hands free for food handling.

Kangaroo rats and pocket mice differ in size (kangaroo rats are much bigger) and in the degree to which they are specialized for bipedal locomotion. These morphological differences seem to be related to the way in which the two kinds of animals exploit the seed bank. Kangaroo rats forage by preference on accumulations of seeds, so that the animal can stop at a seed cache and pick up a relatively large number of items. The rat then moves rapidly over areas—perhaps between shrubs—where seeds are sparsely distributed, stopping at a place where another seed accumulation is detected. In this way, the rat spends relatively little time in traveling and a relatively great amount of time in actually harvesting seeds. Because of this arrangement of its use of time, the kangaroo rat can afford to be choosy in the seeds that it picks up, and it tends to be somewhat of a dietary specialist. Pocket mice, on the other hand, are slower, both because they are smaller and because they are less bipedal; thus, they avoid traversing large open areas where they could be exposed to predation. Instead, they spend most of their time under the cover of shrubs. There, they may encounter pockets of seeds, as do the kangaroo rats, but because they cannot afford to travel long distances from rich pocket to rich pocket they are more likely to take everything they find, even spending time in harvesting solitary seeds, those that are dispersed singly through the soil. Although these modes of foraging are by no means mutually exclusive, pocket mice tend to exploit single seeds, while kangaroo rats seek packets.

The small size of pocket mice has thermoregulatory consequences that affect their annual cycle. When food is scarce or the temperature is low, the smaller of these little rodents may find it too costly to remain active in foraging. In such cases, the animals become torpid and may remain so for varying periods of time. It may be that some of the smaller species of pocket mice become torpid on a daily basis when they encounter energetic problems; and certainly many species are known to become inactive for periods during the colder months of the year. In contrast, kangaroo rats remain active throughout the year, essentially regardless of environmental conditions.

Like their relatives the pocket gophers, heteromyids tend to be aggressive and antisocial. For the most part adult individuals live alone, probably defending at least their burrow systems against other individuals of their species. So pronounced is this solitary tendency in some species of kangaroo rat that the sexes barely tolerate each other except for a very brief period when the female is in estrus and copulation takes place. Some species may have lower levels of aggressiveness, which enable individuals to grow to tolerate each other in captivity; in such cases, however, the female may go into a long period of anestrus, that is, her estrus cycling may cease. For at least some of these animals, then, the solitary life is essential to normal reproduction.

Mating may take place almost throughout the year in some species, while it may be restricted to a certain season in others. Gestation in all heteromyids for which data are available is in the range from twenty-six to thirty days. Litters tend to be small, averaging three to six babies for pocket mice and two to three for kangaroo rats. The young remain in the burrow until they are nearly full size, which is reached probably at the age of one to two months, depending on the species, although this information is in very short supply. Unlike rodents of the family Cricetidae, most heteromyids that are observed above ground, or out of the nest, are nearly adult in physical configuration. For some species of kangaroo rat, it has been shown that peaks in reproductive activity are reached when the animals are eating a large amount of fresh green vegetation. In most parts of the Southwest, such times would coincide with a rainy season, which would be followed by a time of maximum seed production and hence be a suitable time for recruitment of young animals to the population.

Even though litter sizes of heteromyids are relatively small, and their breeding season may be limited, they may sometimes appear in incredible numbers. Several workers from the Museum of Southwestern Biology caught 127 silky pocket mice by hand in two hours of hunting during one August night on the mesa west of Albuquerque; and a student from the University of New Mexico recorded pocket-mouse population densities of thirty per acre in the same general area. Nonetheless, it is not clear that the population fluctuations of these animals are all to be attributed to high reproductive efforts followed by high mortality of the young. Animals sequestering hoards of seeds have the option of remaining underground for long periods of time during stressful weather or when foraging for more food is not profitable; hence, the variations in numbers observed by naturalists may reflect, in part, periods of the animals' activity and inactivity. As with the desert plants that produce huge seed banks with the ability to lie low between the rare periods favorable for growth and reproduction, heteromyids may also tend to keep a low profile over prolonged periods of drought, only to emerge and breed when the rains come. Such a survival strategy calls for a potentially long life span. There is not much information on this point, although some kangaroo rats are known to survive for three years in nature, and a pet *Dipodomys ordii* remained vigorous for ten years.

KANGAROO RATS

Dipodomys

No other small mammal in New Mexico could be mistaken for a kangaroo rat. Jumping mice, *Zapus*, also have elongate hind feet and tails, but they have naked soles, no hip stripe, and an essentially hairless tail, while the tail of *Dipodomys* is well haired and provided with a long terminal tuft. Kangaroo rats may often be seen at night in the headlights of a car if one drives slowly along unused roads through sandy grassland or desert country. They often seem to seek out the tire tracks of these roads as places to forage for accumulated seeds. Sometimes the animals enter the circle of light around a desert campfire and pursue their activities untroubled by the humans who may be present. It is possible to slowly approach a foraging kangaroo rat and then with a quick pounce to catch it by hand. If you miss the first time, however, you are in for a wild chase. Even newly captured *Dipodomys* are relatively gentle, and with a little care, they may be handled quite easily and make attractive pets. A pet kangaroo rat however, is an item only for the night owl, since the animals tend to be almost exclusively nocturnal, preferring to hide and sleep during the day. Examination of the surface of a sandy desert area in the morning often reveals the distinctive tracks of these animals, characterized by imprints of the long hind feet and the marks where the tail has dragged, or where caches of seeds have been excavated. Moonlight may cause the animals to restrict their activity to the shade of shrubs or to remain in their burrows. However, when food is scarce and the nights grow short in spring, the moon ceases to have an effect, and some animals may even search for food in the daytime.

There are three species of *Dipodomys* in New Mexico. All are readily identified, although two, the Merriam kangaroo rat, *D. merriami,* and the Ord kangaroo rat, *D. ordii,* are difficult to separate unless they are examined at very close range. Most distinctive is the bannertail kangaroo rat, *D. spectabilis,* because the terminal one-third of its tail is white, unlike the other species which have brownish or grayish color extending to the tailtip. The two smaller species are very much alike in appearance. However, the Ord rat has five hindtoes per foot, while the Merriam rat has but four. While this may sound like a clear-cut difference, the fifth toe on the Ord rat, corresponding to the big toe in a human, is very tiny and can only be seen after careful examination. Obviously, such a feature is of little use in identifying a kangaroo rat fleeing in the desert. There are some habitat differences between the two; and while they overlap in geographic distribution, there are parts of the state where only the Ord, not the Merriam, is found. *D. ordii* is found in all the grassland and desert areas of the state. However, *D. merriami* is limited to more southern areas: in the Rio Grande Valley, from about Albuquerque southward, and in the Pecos Valley south of Santa Rosa. Where the two species are found together, the Ord rat is most common in sandy areas, while the Merriam is more apt to occur on desert pavements or harder soils in general. The Merriam rat does perfectly well in sandy places, but when the Ord is present it may exclude the Merriam from these more favored habitats. Bannertails are found in most desert and grassland areas of the state, but they seem to have a preference for areas where grass is readily available. This species cuts and harvests the ripe seed heads of various grasses, packs the sheaves into its pouches, and transports them to its burrow system for storage. The burrow of the bannertail is quite distinctive. It is located beneath a large and conspicuous mound, six feet or more in diameter, which was formed by the excavation of the system. There may be several entrances on the surface of the mound, connecting to tunnels and chambers which may descend six feet or more in depth. Within this complex system a single rat lives and stores its food. Unlike the burrows of many species of heteromyid, those of *spectabilis* are not necessarily closed during the day. From the mound small trails radiate in various directions, providing unimpeded access to the foraging areas of the resident. Each individual seems to exclude other bannertails from an area of approximately .05 hectare surrounding the mound. In one area near Socorro approximately 2.5 mounds per hectare were counted, and it was found that the mounds are regularly spaced throughout the habitat, not scattered at random as one would expect if each rat paid no attention to the location of others when it constructed its home. When a rat dies or moves away, the burrow may be occupied by another rat or by any of a variety of other animals that like to live underground, such as burrowing owls, rabbits, ground squirrels, weasels, snakes, or kit foxes. Thus, the burrow systems may persist for several generations before they deteriorate, and the location of an old burrow is still readily detected because the plants that colonize an abandoned site are distinctive.

All kangaroo rats like to take dust baths. In bathing, the animal rolls in the dust, shaking it through the fur. A captive animal which is not given an opportunity to dust bathe quickly becomes disreputable in appearance, with greasy and matted fur. Much of the grease is produced by distinctive mid-dorsal sebaceous glands. Once a rat has bathed at a given site, the deposited secretions tend to attract other rats to bathe in the same place. Thus, dust-bathing sites tend to be communal, and may have some function in integrating the social life, such as it is, of all the rats in the neighborhood.

Kangaroo rats, like most small rodents, have many predators. Owls take many, as do kit foxes, weasels, badgers, ringtail cats, bobcats, and snakes. *Dipodomys* has little economic importance for humans, although bannertails, because of their predilection for grass, may compete to some extent with domestic livestock.

POCKET MICE

Perognathus and *Chaetodipus*

The seven species of New Mexican pocket mice have been divided into two genera. Silky pocket mice belong to the genus *Perognathus*, which includes the species *flavus* and *flavescens*. These species are very small, often weighing only 5 to 6 grams, have conspicuous buff-colored patches behind their ears, and tails not provided with any long hairs.

They tend to be tan, buff, or salmon-colored above and contrastedly white below. Hairy-tailed or spiny pocket mice are placed in the genus *Chaetodipus*, which includes the species *penicillatus, intermedius, nelsoni,* and *baileyi*. These are somewhat larger than the silkies, and have tufts of long hairs on the ends of their tails. These mice tend to be gray above and whitish below. The hispid pocket mouse, *Perognathus hispidus*, is the largest of all, and has a tail and a color pattern somewhat like a silky, but in other ways is like a spiny pocket mouse.

Silky pocket mice, *Perognathus*, live in deserts and grasslands on sandy or gravelly soils, and may be found as high as the piñon-juniper woodland. They may be found in the same places as spiny mice, but are often found in grasslands devoid of shrubs, and such places tend not to be frequented by the larger species. Both species of silky pocket mice are found in most parts of the state, but *flavus* is more abundant and *flavescens* tends to be uncommon in the southern counties. At White Sands National Monument, *P. flavescens* has evolved a whitish local race, presumably in response to the selective pressure exerted by predators on darker-colored mice against the white background. The two kinds are very difficult to distinguish. *Perognathus flavescens* is somewhat larger and relatively longer-tailed, has shorter ear patches (post-auricular patches), and usually is paler in color with fewer black hairs intermixed with the tan of the back than *P. flavus*. Where both species are found in the same place, *flavescens* tends to prefer sandy areas, while *flavus* is more likely to be found on tighter, better-stabilized soils.

Hairy-tailed pocket mice, genus *Chaetodipus*, are found mostly in the southern part of the state, with the northernmost colonies found in lava beds in Bernalillo and southern Sandoval counties. These animals are longer-tailed than the silkies, and they are more adept at climbing, often gathering food in low shrubs such as mesquite. They are predominantly shrub desert inhabitants, prominent members of the terrestrial small mammal communities of southern Arizona, California, and Mexico. As with the silky mice, the species are quite difficult to distinguish. Two kinds, *P. intermedius* and *P. nelsoni*, are known as rock pocket mice. Both kinds are almost always found among the rocks on rocky hillsides. Both kinds are characterized by long, stiff, spinelike hairs extending above the level of the more normal hairs on the rump region. Sometimes these hairs are quite conspicuous, but in young or molting animals they may not be evident. The two kinds are mutually exclusive geographically in our state; *nelsoni* has been recorded only in the Carlsbad area, while *intermedius* is common in rocky desert areas from Sandoval County southward in the Rio Grande drainage and points west. Little is known of the habits of the rock pocket mice. The Bailey pocket mouse, *P. baileyi,* and the desert pocket mouse, *P. penicillatus,* lack rump spines. Bailey's mouse is somewhat longer-tailed and larger, and in our state it has been detected only in the Peloncillo Mountains along the Arizona state line in Hidalgo County. The desert mouse is widespread in low deserts across southern New Mexico, often seeming to prefer mesquite stands.

The hispid pocket mouse, *P. hispidus,* seems most common in the plains regions of eastern New Mexico, although it is also distributed across the southern half of the state in areas of medium to tall grasses or tall annual forbs.

Silky pocket mice readily become torpid when stressed by low temperatures or by lack of food, and they may spend some time in torpor. It is not at all clear that the hairy-tailed pocket mice employ this strategy.

Beaver

Castor canadensis.   Beavers are large brown rodents, weighing up to fifty pounds, with broad flattened tails and webbed hind feet. They are unlikely to be mistaken for any other kind of mammal in New Mexico. Muskrats, *Ondatra zibethicus,* are similarly shaped and colored, and are often seen swimming in ponds and streams; but they are much smaller, at most two to three pounds, and their tails are laterally compressed so that they are higher than wide. The nutria (*Myocastor coypus*) is also beaverlike in appearance, but it is not so large, weighing fifteen to twenty pounds, and has a rounded rather than a flattened or compressed tail. Nutrias are known only from one or two places in southern New Mexico, while beavers are found in much of the state.

Beavers are dependent upon the existence of permanent bodies of water for their survival. They typically inhabit mountain streams in the West, but are also found along the larger lowland rivers. The social unit in beaver life, known as a colony, consists of four to eight related individuals, probably dominated by an adult female, although in some cases a male may be dominant. Once a year, the mature female produces several young, known as kits, after a gestation of about 107 days. The kits are born fully furred with the eyes partially open, and the incisor teeth erupted. Accounts as to duration of dependency on the mother suggest a period of six weeks to three months. The animals may continue to grow for several years; they become sexually mature in their second year. There is some evidence that the presence of a mature female in a colony inhibits sexual maturity in younger females in the group. Much evidence suggests that the dominant male and female animal in a colony form a monogamous pair.

A typical beaver shelter or lodge is a structure made of sticks and mud in a shallow pond or lake. The lodge consists of a broad base of wood and a dome-shaped emergent part within which is a living chamber with a floor elevated several inches above water. One or more entrances are under water. The lodge protects the animals from predators, especially in the winter when bears or coyotes may approach the house across the ice. Temperature inside the lodge is much more stable than it is outside, and tends to stay warm in winter, especially when the animals are at home. Lodges are typically placed in ponds created by the beavers through damming of the stream. The dams are likewise constructed of wood and mud, and cause the water to back up, flooding an extensive area. The life of the colony is centered on the lodge and pond.

The pond itself has profound ecological effects on the surrounding habitat. The flooding causes the deaths of some trees. The dead trees, in turn, provide shelter for various birds that otherwise would not inhabit the place. Water-loving plants thrive in and around the pond, and these provide food and shelter for a variety of animals. The retention of water in the pond causes the local water table to rise, enhancing the growth of additional vegetation. The pond and surrounding wet area acts as a reservoir, preventing rapid runoff of water during rains and ensuring that the stream flows steadily throughout the year. The predictable stream flow allows trout to survive, and further downstream, it allows humans to plan agricultural activities. When the pond fills with silt it becomes less useful to the beavers, and eventually the colony may abandon the site and move further up or down stream. The abandoned pond gradually becomes covered with meadow grasses, and the resulting lush open area is productive of protein-rich grasses for cattle and horses. This typical beaver meadow, a distinctive feature of the northern mountains, is referred to in Spanish as a *vega*.

In the early days of American exploration of the Rocky Mountains, the trapping of beaver fur was a principal economic lure. So easy are beaver to locate and trap that by approximately 1900 the animals were largely extirpated from much of the West, including most New Mexican mountain ranges. When the beavers are gone the dams fall into disrepair, the ponds disappear, and the water table falls. Stream and pondside vegetation dies, and the animals that depend on that habitat leave or become extinct. The vegas are no longer good grazing land,

and the area looses its value for man. The summer rains, unchecked by the dams, cut deeply into the soil and wash it away. Soon, instead of a fertile riparian community, the streamsides are rock-strewn arroyos that hold water only during occasional floods. Downstream, the farmers leave, now that their irrigation water is a thing of the past. The effect of the uncontrolled commercial exploitation of beaver was a classic example of the public and environmental cost of private enterprise. Because the beavers are so obviously beneficial, they were wisely reintroduced to most of the suitable habitats throughout the state and are now widespread.

In lowland areas, where they occur along rivers and drainage canals, beavers may give up houses in favor of bank burrows which they dig.

Beavers are exclusively vegetarian in diet. A favorite food item is the cambial, or growing, layer of tissue just under the bark of shrubs and trees. Many of the trees that are cut are stripped of bark on the spot, or carried to the pond for storage under water as a winter food cache. Buds and roots are also consumed, and when they are needed, a variety of plant species are accepted. There are definite preferences, however, and aspen and willow are high on the beaver's list of favorites. The animals may travel some distance from water to secure food. When a rich food source is exploited, canals may be dug from the pond to the pasture to facilitate the transportation of the items to the beavers' homes.

Activity is mostly carried out during the hours of darkness, but the beavers are abroad before it is completely dark, and they may be seen cruising about in their ponds in early evening. One of the common signs of the presence of beaver is the loud sound made when the tail is slapped on the surface of the water. The sound is frequently made when the animals are disturbed by the presence of humans, and it has been assumed to be a warning to other members of the colony. Beavers also communicate with each other by touch, and by smell. Both sexes possess paired anal scent glands called castors. Secretions from these glands are deposited at various scent posts within the animal's home range, and may have the function of advertising the territory of the colony.

Much of the food ingested by a beaver consists of cellulose, which is normally indigestible by mammals. However, these animals have colonies of microorganisms living in the cecum, a pouch between the large and small intestine, and these symbionts digest up to 30 percent of the cellulose that the beaver takes in. An additional recycling of plant food occurs when certain fecal pellets are eaten and run through the digestive process a second time.

NEW WORLD RATS AND MICE

Family Cricetidae

This is a huge family with many genera and species in both the Old World and the New, including hamsters and gerbils as well as the various species of native deer mice, harvest mice, and wood rats. A group so large is difficult to characterize simply, and specialists are still not in agreement as to the limits of the family. However, within our borders the situation is more manageable. New Mexican cricetids are harvest mice (*Reithrodontomys*, three species), deer mice (*Peromyscus*, nine species), pygmy mice (*Baiomys*, one species), grasshopper mice (*Onychomys*, three species), cotton rats (*Sigmodon*, three species), and woodrats (*Neotoma*, five species). Most of these animals are relatively long-tailed, large-eared, big-eyed rats and mice. They resemble Old World rats and mice (family Muridae), which in our area are represented by the house mouse and Norway and black rats, all introduced by man. These three tend to have nearly naked tails on which the scaly skin is clearly visible; their fur is usually gray or blackish without a sharply two-toned color pattern; and they are distinctive in the structure of their molar teeth. Murids are usually, but not always, found in urban or farm situations, or at least around human habitations. Cricetids may also be seen in these places. Most cricetids are sharply two-toned, with brownish, buff, or gray color dorsally, and white ventrally. One species of cotton rat (*S. fulviventer*) is buff ventrally. Cricetids could be confused with some voles (family Arvicolidae), but voles are short-tailed and short-eared and have relatively small eyes. Voles also tend to be only weakly bicolored, and they are usually darker colored dorsally than most cricetids. Again, the structure of the molar teeth separates the two families.

Among cricetids, harvest mice are easily separable because their upper incisor teeth each have a deep longitudinal groove on the front surface. These are very small mice, with long tails, big ears, small eyes, and a typically bicolored pattern.

The pygmy mouse is even smaller than the harvest mice, but it lacks the incisor grooves, is usually gray dorsally, and is restricted to Hidalgo County in New Mexico.

Cotton rats are medium-sized and dark dorsally, with ears that are partly hidden in the very long fur. They are usually found in areas of tall grass.

Wood rats (also referred to as pack rats) are large, as large as laboratory rats or larger, and they are sharply bicolored, short-furred, large-eared, and large-eyed rodents. Their long tail is well haired and usually bicolored as well. They are most often found in woodlands and in rocky terrain, sometimes in mountain cabins.

Grasshopper mice have short, fat tails, but in other respects they fit the cricetid mold quite well. They are usually found in desert areas.

Deer mice are small, somewhat larger than a harvest mouse but much smaller than a wood rat. They are the prototypic "pop-eyed field mice," with large protruding black eyes, huge ears, and an attractive bicolored pattern. In woodland and forest areas these are sometimes the most abundant small mammals, and they may also be quite common in grasslands and in deserts.

Identification of all these cricetids is greatly facilitated by examination of a cleaned skull, and the appropriate technical skull characteristics are described in the key.

With such a large group of animals, it is not surprising that it is difficult to generalize about habits. However, the majority of cricetids are alike in being nocturnal (cotton rats are an exception), and in tending to forage in the open, often climbing over rocks and low shrubs, not confining their activity to tunnels or runways (again, cotton rats are an exception). It seems likely that the build and color of the cricetids are related to this mode of foraging. Bicoloration, or "countershading" as it is called, is a pattern used by organisms exposed to light from above, such as moonlight. The darker top of the animal is lightened by the incident light; and the shadow cast by the animal's body, which might make it conspicuous to a predator, is lightened by the whitish undersides. The net result is that the animal is rendered relatively inconspicuous. Perhaps significantly, the one group of cricetids not strongly bicolored, the cotton rats, spend a good deal of their above-ground time in foraging in runways, which they construct through the grass, and as a result, they are not frequently exposed to view. Elongate tails have been shown to enhance a small mammal's ability to climb; indeed, there is a direct relationship between relative tail length and the fraction of foraging time spent in climbing. Large eyes are useful to a nocturnal animal that sees by the faint light available in the open, even on a very dark night. The large, mobile ears of cricetids are constantly at work in gathering sound from all directions, an ability greatly reduced in such animals as arvicolids, in which large external ears would be an impediment in dwelling in tunnels.

Cricetids are generalists in diet, consuming a variety of plant and animal foods. However, the bulk of the food of most species consists of the reproductive parts of plants, such as flowers and the various kinds of fruits.

HARVEST MICE

Reithrodontomys

Harvest mice are common in most habitats in New Mexico from the level of the ponderosa forest downward through low deserts. They may be found in much higher elevations, however, and have been taken in open meadows in the spruce-fir forest on Sandía Crest. These tiny mice often build nests of grass and other fibrous vegetation, which they place on the surface of the ground, under a shelter such as a rock or log, or even a foot or two above ground level in a small shrub. The living chamber in the nest is lined with softer material, such as milkweed or cottonwood down. One or two openings from below give access to the inner chamber. The mice are quite tolerant of each other, and it is not uncommon to find two or more sharing a nest. This sharing may have important energetic consequences. Mammals as small as harvest mice (10–15 grams) lose heat rapidly, even when well insulated, and it has been shown that when several harvest mice huddle together in the shelter of a nest, energy loss for heating purposes may be cut by 25 percent or more. When stressed by low temperatures in the laboratory or in a live trap, the little animals may become torpid by lowering their body temperatures by one-third of their active temperature. However, it is not known if the mice enter torpidity in nature. Each animal forages in a home range of somewhat less than a half-acre, but so far as is known, they do not defend territories. In fact, it has been suggested that the fulvous harvest mouse, *R. fulvescens,* may form monogamous pair bonds. The western harvest mouse, *R. megalotis,* has returned to its home territory from an experimental displacement of as much as one thousand feet. The foraging area of a harvest mouse is distinctly three dimensional because most individuals are very scansorial (well adapted for climbing in low vegetation). In one study, more than half of the animals captured were taken in live traps placed on platforms a meter above the ground.

Females may bear their first litter at the age of twelve weeks, follow this with a postpartum estrus, and continue to bear young throughout the warmer months of the year. Captive females have produced as many as fifty-eight young in a single year. Two to six young are born after a gestation of twenty-three to twenty-four days. The babies are altricial but grow rapidly, and are weaned in twenty-four days. Senility begins at about forty-five weeks, and it is likely that the population is completely renewed each year. Population densities have been estimated to be from two to thirty animals per acre.

The diet varies seasonally, with insects commonly eaten in early summer, and seeds predominating in fall and winter. It has been calculated that the cost of heating one western harvest mouse for one night in California is about 3½ grains of wheat.

Three species are found in New Mexico. All are similar to each other, but one, the fulvous harvest mouse, *R. fulvescens,* has been taken only in the Peloncillo Mountains of Hidalgo County; and one, the plains harvest mouse, *R. montanus,* is quite rare, comprising only 2 percent of all the harvest mice examined by workers at the Museum of Southwestern Biology. The third species is the western harvest mouse, *R. megalotis.* It is often abundant and is found in most habitats throughout the state.

DEER MICE

Peromyscus

One or another species of deer mouse is found in almost every terrestrial habitat in North America. Often the local species of *Peromyscus* is the most common mammal. In New Mexico, *Peromyscus* is found from the alpine regions down into the driest desert areas. Along this transect, rocky foothills in the lower ponderosa forest and in the woodland seem favored by deer mice, and in this zone so many as four or even five species may coexist in the same general area. Lower, in grassland or desert, or higher, in mixed coniferous or spruce-fir forest, it is unusual to find more than one common species of deer mice. Where more than one species is found in a local situation, there is usually a certain amount of habitat separation. For example, in the Sandía foothills near Albuquerque, the white-footed mouse, *P. leucopus,* is found in the arroyo bottoms and edges; the brush mouse, *P. boylii,* is found on the south-facing hillsides among oaks and beargrass; and the piñon mouse, *P. truei,* is found on north-facing slopes in piñon-juniper woodland. In southern New Mexican desert ranges, the cactus mouse, *P. eremicus,* is found on the bajadas, in the canyon bottoms, and on south-facing slopes; while the brush mouse inhabits oak groves on north slopes and in other cooler places. In mixed coniferous and spruce-fir forest, the deer mouse, *P. maniculatus,* is usually the only *Peromyscus,* while in most grasslands and in those deserts which lack mesquite, *P. leucopus* or *P. maniculatus* prevails.

Peromyscus populations may be very high, but they tend to fluctuate throughout the season, with a peak in late summer or fall and a low point in late winter and spring. The females are polyestrous in captivity, with an estrus cycle lasting about five days. In the wild, reproduction may cease in winter or at other unfavorable seasons. Gestation has been estimated at twenty-one to twenty-eight days, with the longer times possibly attributed to a delay in implantation of the embryo in the uterine wall of a female still nursing young from a previous litter. One to ten young, with an average of three or four, are born in a hairless, blind condition. Growth is rapid and the babies are weaned at three to four weeks. Females may enter their first estrus at this time, but the onset of reproductive activity usually occurs after five to six weeks. The litter size of the female increases with each birth, peaking at the fifth or sixth litter, and declines thereafter. While they are still helpless, the babies must be transported by the mother while they are fastened to her nipples. Wild *Peromyscus leucopus* have been known to survive twenty-two months, but a much shorter life span is more usual. The young animals may remain with the mother for some time after they are weaned. Most deer mice are rather tolerant of each other, and, especially in winter, several animals may occupy the same nest, probably in part to conserve heat. Each adult animal may occupy a home range of one-tenth acre to as much as ten acres, but there is relatively little evidence to suggest that territories are defended. Home ranges of male cactus mice have been found to overlap, while those of females do not. Pairing of males and females is probably transitory.

Deer mice forage over the ground and also by climbing in shrubs and trees. Longer-tailed species, such as *P. boylii,* may spend a substantial portion of their active time in shrubs and trees. In a study of *leucopus, boylii,* and *truei* in the Cerrillos Hills, it was found that the percentage of foraging time spent on the ground, in shrubs, and in trees was directly correlated with the anatomy of the animals, and differed between the three species. Even among the members of the same species, it was found that longer-tailed individuals spent more time in foraging aloft than shorter-tailed ones. The diet of deer mice varies according to both habitat and season. Insects and other invertebrates are eaten in spring and summer, and seeds are more important later in the year. Some species may store large quantities of seeds, while for others there is no evidence of hoarding. Food or temperature stress may induce torpor, and there is some evidence that periods of torpor may occur in nature. The cactus mouse, for example, may enter torpor on a daily basis, and may become torpid during extended hot dry periods. Most peromyscan activity is nocturnal. Some species may favor periods of moonlight.

Nine species of *Peromyscus* inhabit New Mexico. Three—the deer-mouse (*P. maniculatus*), the white-footed mouse (*P. leucopus*), and the cactus mouse (*P. eremicus*)—have tails that lack a long tuft of hairs extending well beyond the tail tip (such a tail is described as terete). The remaining species have long hairs extending well beyond the tip of the tail sheath (such a tail is described as penicillate). The cactus mouse differs from *leucopus* and *maniculatus* in the soles of its hind feet, which are completely naked. In the other two species, the heel portion of the sole of the hindfoot is covered with hair. These two are distinguished only with difficulty. The white-footed mouse is somewhat larger and occurs in arroyos, lowland valleys, and grasslands. The deer mouse is found throughout the forested regions, in grasslands, and occasionally in the desert. The penicillate-tailed species differ from each other chiefly in the relative lengths of tail and ears. The canyon mouse, *P. crinitus,* has a very hairy, almost bushy tail and a bright buffy dorsal coloration, and it is limited to boulder piles at the foot of cliffs in the piñon-juniper zone of San Juan and McKinley counties. The white-ankled mouse, *P. pectoralis,* has its ankles completely covered with white hairs, and is limited to the Carlsbad Cavern region in Eddy County. The remaining species have the dark coloration of the dorsal part of the shank extending over the ankle joint. These four—*truei, difficilis, gratus,* and *boylii*—differ in ear size (with *truei* the largest, *boylii* the smallest) and in tail length (*truei* is the shortest, *difficilis* the longest); but aside from resorting to careful measurement of specimens, they are best distinguished by habitat. *Peromyscus truei* and *gratus* are most common in piñon-juniper wood-land, with *gratus* replacing *truei* west of the Rio Grande and south of Interstate-40. *P. boylii* is a mouse of the live oak woodland and brushy hillsides. *P. difficilis* seems to prefer jumbles of large rocks in woodland or below, and is often common in fields of lava boulders. The common names of these species—piñon, brush, and rock mouse, respectively—reflect these habitat preferences. In the course of the 1975 survey of the mammals of New Mexico, workers from the Museum of Southwestern Biology examined 7,422 specimens of *Peromyscus*. The relative numbers of the eight species recognized at that time give an idea of their abundance within our borders:

maniculatus	45%
boylii	20%
truei (including *gratus*)	10%
leucopus	9%
eremicus	7%
difficilis	7%
crinitus	1%
pectoralis	1%

Pygmy Mouse

Baiomys taylori. These tiny mice (7 to 8 grams), limited in their occurrence to southern Hidalgo County, resemble a small juvenile *Peromyscus* or *Reithrodontomys*. What little is known about their habits, however, suggests that they are not merely miniatures of those genera. Pygmy mice apparently construct runways through the dense grass in which they live, and in this way, they are like voles (arvicolids) rather than other cricetids. Moreover, observations of captive animals indicate that the males take part in caring for the young, again unlike *Peromyscus* or *Reithrodontomys*. Females in captivity produce litters containing from one to five young (averaging three) every twenty-five to thirty-one days. The gestation period is calculated to be from twenty to twenty-three days, and is probably prolonged in nursing females. Young animals seemingly remain fastened to the nipples of the female until weaning at eighteen to twenty-two days. Females may reach puberty at twenty-eight days and produce their first litter as early as sixty-four days after birth, but the average age of first litter production is eighty-two days. A postpartum estrus is common. At the age of fifty days young *Baiomys* have essentially attained adult size. Pygmy mice have often been noted to be active during the afternoon and early evening. Some evidence suggests that they may consume more of the vegetative part of plants than do *Peromyscus*.

GRASSHOPPER MICE

Onychomys

Grasshopper mice resemble deer mice, but they are stockier and have short, fat tails that are only about half the length of the head and body. Close examination reveals other differences, including the un-usually elongate front claws.

These are mice of deserts and grasslands. In exceptional cases, they may be found in woodland or forest regions. *Onychomys* is distinctive among cricetines because its diet includes a high percentage of animal prey, such as a variety of arthropods and even a few vertebrates. These mice have developed specialized killing techniques, even for dangerous prey such as scorpions, which sometimes comprise an important part of the menu. Pocket mice may be killed by a bite through the spinal cord behind the cranium. As partial carnivores, grasshopper mice tend to be less common than other desert mice, and they seem to maintain some-what more stable population levels. Approximately one *Onychomys* per acre has been calculated in one study.

A typical social unit inhabiting one burrow system may consist of an adult male and female and their young. The males are highly ter-ritorial among themselves, and advertise their areas by high-pitched vocalizations consisting of a long monotonous keening. The "howling" of *Onychomys* is a sound familiar to the perceptive desert camper. The hunting territory of the family unit may be up to eight acres or more.

The gestation of *Onychomys* has been estimated to be from twenty-seven to thirty-eight days. Longer periods have been attributed to the delay caused by lactation in the females, but there seems to be no evidence of delayed implantation of the embryos, and the mechanism behind the longer gestations remains unclear. One to seven young comprise a litter, with the average size ranging from three to four. Males aid females in caring for the young, which are weaned by twenty to twenty-three days. Age at sexual maturity is greater for males than for females, and seems to be greater for the northern grasshopper mouse (*O. leucogaster*) than for the southern (*O. arenicola*). *O. arenicola* females may begin breeding activity at eight weeks, while females of *O. leucogaster* are generally not ready until the twelfth or thirteenth week of life. Captive females have produced up to fifty-two young per year, and the lifetime expectation of an individual has been estimated to be eighty-three young. While captives may breed throughout the year, wild animals cease breeding during the winter months.

The two common species in New Mexico are the northern, *O. leucogaster*, and the southern, *O. arenicola*. The two are quite similar, but *arenicola* is a bit smaller and has a slightly longer tail. Where the two are found in proximity, *leucogaster* prefers sandy areas, while *arenicola* may be found on the desert pavements of bajadas and other more obdurate soils. A third species, *O. torridus*, which is widespread in southern

Arizona, has been detected just inside the state line in Hidalgo County. It is very similar to *O. arenicola* and is told apart chiefly on the basis of cytological characteristics.

COTTON RATS

Sigmodon

Cotton rats are inhabitants of grasslands where the species of grasses involved are tall and provide good cover. Generally, the rats are found below the woodlands, although the yellow-nosed cotton rats, *S. ochrognathus*, may be found in open pine forests. During times of population highs, the animals may disperse into a variety of less suitable habitats. Typically, *Sigmodon* makes runways through the grass, where it spends much of its traveling time. Where open space occurs between the bunches of grass, the animals may transit such clearings rapidly, preferring the shelter of the clumps. Burrows are dug, and nests may be constructed on the surface of the ground or in burrows.

The animals may be active anytime during the day or night, but typically they show periods of high and low activity. Breeding may take place throughout the year in the laboratory, but it is generally seasonal in our area, with annual peaks in the late summer or fall. One to fifteen young are born after a gestation period of twenty-seven to thirty-five days. The average number of young in several studies varied between seven and nine. Unlike the young of other New Mexican cricetines, baby *Sigmodon* are fully furred, able to walk, and open their eyes within eighteen to thirty-six hours. They are weaned in ten to fifteen days. In captivity females conceive as early as thirty-eight days of age, while males may not produce sperm until they are from sixty-nine to ninety days old. Young animals are essentially adult in skeletal growth after one hundred days. Once mature, females have an estrous cycle of eight to nine days. In one study, the average life expectancy for animals caught in the wild averaged two months.

Populations may grow as large as thirty to thirty-five per acre, but the animals may essentially vanish from large areas during population lows, when they have been recorded at densities of less than one animal per four acres of habitat. Each individual has a home range of 0.1 to 0.2 acres in good habitat, but this figure must change with changes in density. Little is known of social life. Pairing has been said to be transitory in the wild, although pairs form in the laboratory.

Three species occur in New Mexico. The tawny-bellied cotton rat, *S.*

fulviventer, differs from the other two in its ventral surface, which is a rich buffy color contrasting with the blackish or dark brown dorsal surface of the animal. This species is found in the Rio Grande Valley and in the grasslands of southwestern New Mexico. The yellow-nosed cotton rat, *S. ochrognathus,* has a light-colored belly, and a buffy or yellowish wash on the nose and facial region. It is limited to southern Hidalgo County. Most common is the hispid cotton rat, *S. hispidus,* which is light-bellied and lacks the yellowish nose and face. *S. hispidus* is found in the grasslands of southern and eastern New Mexico. All three species may inhabit the same kinds of habitats; but where *fulviventer* and *hispidus* coexist, the former prefers more dense and undisturbed grasslands, while the latter is more common in disturbed places. Where the three species occur in Hidalgo County, *S. ochrognathus* is most likely to be found in hillside stands of bunch grass, agaves, prickly pears, oaks, and other shrubs, while the other two species occupy the grasslands at lower elevations.

WOOD RATS

Neotoma

These are large rats with strikingly bicolored pelage, long tails, large naked ears, and large eyes. Wood rats are among the most characteristic small mammals of the West, with one or another species living in every habitat from the alpine regions to the lowest deserts. Cotton rats are smaller, have shorter ears, are not distinctly brown or gray above and white below, and possess hairy rather than mostly naked ears. Norway and black rats (*Rattus*) are not strikingly bicolored.

Most wood rats have a strongly developed habit of building nests in large accumulations of material which they assemble around the base of a shrub or tree, in a rock crevice or among boulders, or even in a human habitation. These conspicuous nests tend to be constructed of portable materials that are handy within the rat's home range. Sometimes, while carrying a stick or cactus joint back to its house, a rat may encounter another item which it favors, and drop the first item to pick up the second. If the favored item happens to be a piece of silverware or clothing in a cabin, the rat may convey the impression that it has traded one item for another; hence the name "trade rat" is sometimes used. The habit of assembling huge accumulations of material has also led to the name "pack rat," probably the most commonly heard English name for these rodents in the West.

Each wood rat nest is occupied by one adult *Neotoma*, which may be a female with young. Adult individuals are mutually intolerant in the wild, although they may rarely become accustomed to each other in captivity. Males are especially aggressive toward other males, but even males and females show scant acceptance of each other except when the female is in estrus. This antisocial behavior leads to the defense of an area around the house by its resident. If the resident dies or moves away, the house may be reoccupied, especially if it is a good one in a favorable locality. Pack-rat houses may be continuously occupied for years, and even when they are finally abandoned, they are extremely slow to deteriorate. *Neotoma* dens thousands of years old have been discovered in the Southwest, and provide a fascinating insight into the local vegetation extant in the area at the time that the nest was constructed. Other animals may take advantage of the ready-made shelter, even when the owner is in residence. Other rodents, rabbits, shrews, snakes, lizards, and a variety of invertebrates may share the structure with the rat.

Females are seasonally polyestrus. In our area, the five-day estrus cycle continues from about January or February until August, depending upon elevation and latitude. Gestation has been estimated at twenty-seven to thirty-eight days in various western species; and unlike the situation in many rodents, it has been suggested that nursing does not prolong gestation in this genus. One to six young may make up a litter, but the most common number is rather low: two in the white-throated woodrat (*N. albigula*). The mother enters estrus immediately after bearing a litter, and may thus produce two or more litters per season. Like many other cricetids, baby pack rats tend to spend much of their time tightly affixed to the mother's nipples, and they may be dragged from the nest in this fashion if the mother is forced to flee. The young are weaned at four to six weeks, but they may remain with the mother for some time, and may even attempt to nurse after the next litter has arrived. Full adult size is not attained until about the eighth month. The bushy-tailed wood rat (*N. cinerea*) does not breed until its second year of life, but females of some smaller species have been known to attain reproductive maturity by two to three months of age.

Even though pack rats are territorial, they may attain high population densities in favorable habitats. The white-throated species commonly attains levels of ten per acre, and it has been recorded at highs of over twenty. There is little evidence that *Neotoma* populations fluctuate very much in our region.

Adult wood rats fight with each other a good deal, and signs of this combat are often seen in tattered ears and other scars. The rats are not very vocal, but they do advertise their presence by drumming their hind feet on the ground, and sometimes by vibrating their tails in the vegetation. These animals have scent glands in the skin of the mid-ventral region, and some species have been noted rubbing their bellies on the ground and against various objects in their territories, perhaps to mark and advertise their domain.

Pack rats are chiefly vegetarian, although like most cricetids, they eat some invertebrate animals. The specific diet varies with the species and the availability of different kinds of plants, but all *Neotoma* seem to show a preference for foliage rather than stems, fruits, or flowers. Those species that live in the higher mountains (*cinerea* and *mexicana*) show a strong tendency to accumulate food stores for the winter, while the lowland species (*albigula* and *micropus*) have a lesser tendency to hoard food.

Five species of *Neotoma* inhabit New Mexico. One, the bushy-tail, *N. cinerea*, has a markedly bushy tail, almost like that of a small squir-rel. The other species have short hairs on their tails, but the tail does not appear bushy. The plains wood rat, *N. micropus*, is steel gray dor-sally, even when it is in adult pelage. All of the remaining species are brownish as adults, although the juveniles may be gray. Of the remain-ing three, two—the white-throated, *N. albigula*, and Stephens's wood rat, *N. stephensi*, have throat hairs that are totally white all the way to the base of the hairs; while the Mexican, *N. mexicanus*, has white throat hairs which are lead gray at their base. Stephens's wood rat has a hairier, less bicolored tail than *N. albigula*.

The five species tend to occupy different habitats, and to differ in geographic distribution. The bushy-tail wood rat is confined to higher elevations in the northern mountains and to cliff areas in San Juan County. By preference, they make their nests in vertical fissures in high cliffs, but when necessary, they will occupy other sites. This is the common pack rat of the mountain cabin. The Mexican wood rat is found widely throughout the state, except for the eastern plains region. It tends to prefer heavy vegetative cover, or at least the security of massive accumulations of rocks. It is common in all the montane forests of the state, and may be found at lower elevations if suitable shelter is avail-able. Typical lowland sites are the lava fields at Grants and near Car-rizozo. *Neotoma mexicana* uncommonly builds houses, and is almost never found away from rocks. It feeds chiefly on the foliage of trees, shrubs, and forbs. The white-throated wood rat is the most widespread and common species in New Mexico. It is distributed from the piñon-juniper woodland downward through the desert areas. Although it occupies grassland, it does so only rarely in the eastern part of the state where the plains wood rat is common. The white-throat wood rat may build its nest in rocky areas, but it also nests in the deserts and grasslands where shrubs, small trees, or cacti are available. In such situations, the rats construct their nests around the bases of these plants. This species has overcome the difficulties in dealing with cacti. Not only do the animals nest in cactus thickets, but they climb through the cacti with impunity, gathering the pads or joints for food and leaving the spiny areoles in thick accumulations around their nests, which has the effect of deterring the entrance of mammalian predators. A high proportion, half or more, of the diet of *albigula* is comprised of cacti. Seemingly, the water needs of the rats are met by consuming this succulent plant, and captive animals, provided with succulent vegetation, rarely drink. In those places where tree yuccas (*Yucca elata*) are common, the rats climb the plants and cut the leaves. Sometimes, the continued use of a yucca by the animals results in a pruned runway up the trunk into the foliage. The low-growing *Yucca glauca* is also utilized as food, and it is not unusual to see plants with the leaves neatly clipped off from the ground level upward, leaving a small tuft at the top. Plains wood rats (*N. micropus*) occupy the same habitats as the white-throat wood rat; however, the former species is most common in the eastern plains of New Mexico, and is uncommon in the Rio Grande Valley and the southwestern part of the state. In those places where both the white-throat and the plains species are found together, as in the area between Albuquerque and the Sandía Mountains, the white-throat lives in the rocky foothills and the plains wood rat dwells along arroyos and in the grassland below the piñon-juniper woodland. Stephens's wood rat, *N. stephensi*, is chiefly an inhabitant of the northwestern quarter of the state, west of the Rio Grande and north of the Deming Plain. Its life seems to be closely tied to the existence of juniper. It feeds on these plants and builds nests around and within the trees. This animal also nests in crevices in arroyo banks, and in rocky areas. In those places where *stephensi* and *albigula* occur together, the former tends to live in junipers, while the latter is more tied to rocky situations. In a canyon near Flagstaff, *stephensi* was found living high on the canyon walls in crevices in small rocks in the juniper zone; *albigula* was most common in piles of large rocks at the foot of the cliffs; and *mexicana* occupied piles of large rocks and dense vegetation on the canyon floor.

Wood rats have been raised successfully in captivity, but many individuals never adjust and few become accustomed to handling. They are not good pets, and not very successful laboratory animals.

VOLES

Arvicolidae

To most people a vole is a mouse. To northern European peoples these creatures were originally called *vole-mice*, from a Scandinavian word meaning "field mouse." Indeed, most voles are specialized for life in fields or meadows where their ability to cut runways through the grass and their short-tailed, short-eared, and stocky build fits them to live in these tunnels. Living in runways, the animals are not exposed to view as often as cricetids, and consequently they are less bicolored and smaller-eyed. These features, related to their ecology, serve to distinguish most arvicolids from most cricetids. Small cricetids are more properly called mice. The word *mouse* derives from an old Indo-European stem which applied originally to the house mouse (*Mus*) and its close relatives, and has been transferred to small rodents with a similar long-tailed, big-eared build, such as *Peromyscus* and *Reithrodontomys*. All voles resemble each other in their general build and their lack of pronounced color pattern, but not all are inhabitants of meadows or fields. The muskrat, *Ondatra zibethicus*, is aquatic, and in the Pacific Northwest several species of the genus *Arborimus* are specialized for arboreal life. However, the life of most voles is closely related to the biology of grass. Voles tend to feed on the leaves and stems of grass plants, and thus, they must contend with the tough silicaceous nature of this material. Grass is especially hard to chew and break down mechanically; as a result, the grinding teeth of voles have broad and complex crowns for abrading these obdurate materials. Those species that specialize on grass also tend to have cheek teeth which grow throughout life, so that the wear resulting from chewing can be compensated. Since grass, more than many other kinds of plants, is difficult to digest chemically, voles have an especially enlarged cecum, a dead-end pouch extending from the intestine where the large and small intestines join, and where, with the help of microorganisms, breakdown of the food material may take place. The teeth of mice are simpler, lower-crowned, and do not grow continually; and mice have a small cecum which is not suited to the digestion of grass. Grass is likely to be an unpredictable resource, especially in the arid Southwest where rainfall, at best, is scant and likely not to occur, even in the so-called rainy seasons. Under such conditions grass grows when it rains, and at other times it may be in short supply. An animal whose livelihood depends upon grass must either learn to live on other resources or figure out how to become inactive during the dry spells. Voles have accommodated to this unpredictable existence by developing reproductive cycles that are triggered by the growth of grass. When it rains and the grass grows, the local voles are stimulated by substances in the growing grass plants. Within a few days the females enter estrus, ovulate in response to copulation, become pregnant, and produce a litter of four to six young in about three weeks. The babies are naked and helpless, but they grow very rapidly, and the young females are sexually mature at the age of a month or less. Their brothers mature somewhat later. Immediately after giving birth, the mothers enter estrus and may become inseminated immediately, producing another litter within three more weeks. Such a high biotic potential can lead very quickly to enormous buildups in numbers of voles. The growing grass crop may be exploited fully, with much of its production incorporated into the vole population. The voles are likely to suffer considerable mortality from predation as well as from the adverse effects of overcrowding. Under certain circumstances the populations become so dense that aggressive encounters between individuals interfere with feeding, mating, and care of the young. Many individuals leave, dispersing to less-crowded habitats or sometimes to places that are less than optimal. In northern countries lemmings, which are voles, undergo these dispersal phases periodically, and often with considerable attendant mortality. These movements have been called lemming migrations, but the term *migration* is usually used by biologists to describe a behavior in which the animal goes and also returns on a predictable schedule, as in the case of migratory birds. Voles do not migrate, but they might be said to emigrate from areas of dense populations, much like the exodus of people from crowded countries to North America. Unlike human emigrants, however, most of the voles die before becoming established in the new territory. Emigration, together with the increased death rate in the growing population, eventually brings about a crash in the population. Enough voles have been produced, however, so that a few survive until the grass grows again.

Voles in New Mexico fall into four categories: meadow voles (genus *Microtus*), redback voles (genus *Clethrionomys*), heather voles (genus *Phenacomys*), and the muskrat (*Ondatra zibethicus*). Muskrats are quite large, perhaps a foot long including their tails; they have a long tail, which is scaly and compressed from side to side, and are almost always seen in or near the water. Redback voles in New Mexico are usually found in high mountain forests in northern or western New Mexico; they have a rich reddish back with buffy or whitish underside. Heather voles are rare, and have been reported only from higher elevations in the Sangre de Cristo and San Juan mountains. They resemble meadow voles, from which they are distinguished only with great difficulty. Meadow voles may be quite common in the various mountains of the state, and may be found at lower elevations in the far north. They are typical voles, with short appendages, a stocky body, and brown or blackish coloration.

Muskrat

Ondatra zibethicus.   Muskrats, medium-sized brown animals with a stocky body and long tail, are usually seen swimming in a ditch or beaver pond. They are sometimes incorrectly identified as young beavers, but they differ from the beaver in having a laterally compressed tail rather than a dorsoventrally flattened one.

Muskrats always live in the vicinity of permanent water, a restriction that limits their distribution in New Mexico to the valleys of the major rivers, the San Juan, Rio Grande, and Pecos, and to higher elevations in the mountains where beaver ponds provide a suitable habitat. In these places, the muskrats may live in burrows excavated in the banks of ponds or ditches, or in a house made of water plants which rises above the pond like a small beaver lodge. The houses are based on the bottom of the water body, contain a nest lined with soft vegetation, and are entered by one or more underwater tunnels. Burrows are usually used in streams and ditches, while houses are preferred in beaver ponds, lakes, and marshes. The animals are accomplished swimmers both on the surface and under water. In surface swimming, buoyancy is provided by a layer of air trapped in the woolhairs next to the skin. Over 20 percent of the animal's dry volume is made up of this air layer. *Ondatra* may remain submerged for as long as twenty minutes, though much shorter times are more usual. During dives the heart rate slows down and an oxygen debt is accumulated in the muscles, a situation similar to what is observed in other diving mammals, including humans.

Vegetation makes up a large proportion of the diet, although at times animal matter may be consumed. Most of the plants eaten are water plants available in the foraging range of the muskrat. Animals in the diet include crayfish, fish, and sometimes other small vertebrates.

These animals tend to be antisocial, with the males and females occupying separate territories that are defended more or less vigorously, especially during the breeding season. Competition for choice burrow sites may be intense, and such places are usually occupied by dominant animals. Gestation lasts from twenty-five to thirty days, and four to eight young are born in a blind and hairless condition. The number of young per litter varies with latitude: animals in the north have larger families than those in the south. The number of litters per year also varies latitudinally, but in the opposite way: in Louisiana five to six litters per year are the rule, while in Maine two or three are produced. It is not known if this trend occurs within New Mexico. Young females normally do not breed until the spring following their year of birth, though a few born early in the year may reproduce in the same season. The life span of the animals ranges from two to three years.

Muskrats are normally nocturnal, but at certain seasons they may be seen foraging during the day.

Because of the thickness and fine texture of the fur, these animals are of substantial economic value. The pelts are used to make coats and to line or cover various garments. A properly trimmed muskrat coat resembles mink quite closely, and "mink-dyed muskrat" is sometimes found on the market. Because of their limited distribution, muskrats are not of great economic importance in New Mexico.

Red-Backed Vole

Clethrionomys gapperi.   Few New Mexicans have an opportunity to see red-backed voles. In our state, they are limited in distribution and rather rare because they inhabit moist forests at the highest elevations. In Britain and northern Europe, however, *Clethrionomys* is one of the most common small mammals, as it is in northern parts of North America.

These beautiful rodents are omnivores, although chiefly vegetarian. So far as is known, they have no organized family life. Females become reproductively mature by the age of two to four months, and produce litters of two to eight young after gestations lasting from seventeen to nineteen days. The young are weaned by seventeen days of age. *Clethrionomys* may be better able to deal with low temperatures than some other local voles, and it is known to begin breeding under the snow in early spring.

Heather Vole

Phenacomys intermedius.   This high-elevation vole occurs in a variety of habitats at and above timberline. Few specimens are known from

New Mexico, and little is known of its natural history. *Phenacomys* resembles the montane vole (*Microtus montanus*), but the latter is unknown in the New Mexican Sangre de Cristo range, where the heather vole seems to be most common. A gray short-tailed vole from high in the Sangre de Cristos should be suspected of belonging to this species.

Meadow Voles

Microtus. Meadow voles are most common in open grassy places in montane forests. A requisite for most species is sufficient soil moisture to promote the growth of grass or sedges. If marshy conditions obtain at lower elevations, some voles may be found there as well. Among the New Mexican species there is a gradient in tolerance to dryer conditions. The long-tailed and Pennsylvania voles seem least able to tolerate dry places, while the montane, Mexican, and prairie voles seem more capable of persisting in drier grasslands.

In those places where two or three species occur in close proximity, each may be most common in a different habitat. On a number of mountain ranges, such as the Sandías, Manzanos, Sacramentos, and Mogollons, where the Mexican and long-tailed voles coexist, the former is most common in open or drier grasslands, while the latter prefers forest-edge or interior-forest situations. In the Jemez and San Juan mountains, where the long-tail coexists with the montane vole, the latter occupies habitats usually taken by Mexican voles further south. In the White Mountains, in nearby Arizona, all three species are found together. There, the long-tail is a forest and forest-edge animal; the Mexican occupies drier grasslands; and the montane preempts the most mesic sedge-grass habitats next to the ponds and streams. Pennsylvania voles are almost always found near water in moist grass-sedge habitats. Such places need not be located in the mountains, however. For example, small marshes in the otherwise arid grasslands and woodlands north of the San Juan River shelter small colonies, as does the alkaline marsh in the short-grass prairie near Wagon Mound. Indeed, this species does not ascend to high elevations in New Mexico.

All species of *Microtus* seem to have high reproductive potentials, although the different kinds vary in this regard. Young animals attain sexual maturity at the age of a month or less. Ovulation is induced by copulation, and gestation lasts about twenty-one days. The babies are weaned in two to three weeks, and quickly enter the reproductive population. Those animals born late in the summer or fall may cease growing and pass through the winter at a size smaller than that attained by adults. It has been suggested that these smaller animals are more energy efficient during the colder months. In spring these small individuals quickly attain normal adult size and begin to breed. Most probably live no more than one or two months, and their maximal life span is probably less than a year. Litter size ranges from one to ten or eleven, with the most common size from four to six.

These animals have the capability of producing enormous numbers of young, and under favorable conditons, populations may attain very high levels. High mortality rates can quickly bring their numbers down, and marked highs and lows in populations of *Microtus* are obvious and commonly observed. During highs, the animals may seem to be everywhere in favorable habitats, and they may readily be seen and heard at all times of the day and night. During lows, the mammalogist may hunt for days to find a few specimens for study. These changes are often referred to as cycles, and they do seem to occur over periods of three or four years. However, most population biologists prefer to call the changes fluctuations, since they are not predictably cyclic in nature. Indeed, some *Microtus* living in places where the availability of moisture and suitable grass and sedge is dependable seem not to fluctuate in numbers at all.

Most species of *Microtus* seem to be rather antisocial, with each individual living independently in a foraging area. In some cases, the area may be defended to a certain extent. The prairie vole, however, is highly social and lives in family units consisting of a monogamous pair and their young. Each family has its own home range, but only the nest area is defended and the foraging areas overlap widely. Home ranges of various species vary from one-tenth of an acre to about a half-acre.

All of our species of *Microtus* are chiefly herbivorous, and most feed principally on grasses and sedges—more specifically, on the leaves and stems of the plants. A few species, probably including the long-tailed vole, use many dicotyledonous plants. During times of shortage in the preferred foods, they eat roots, bark, and other less nutritious parts. It has been shown that some species of *Microtus*, including the montane vole, respond to an organic molecule contained in growing grass and other plants by rapid initiation of reproductive activities.

Five species of *Microtus* have been found in New Mexico. All are quite similar in general appearance, and difficult for anyone but a trained mammalogist to identify with certainty. Thus far, the prairie vole, *M. ochrogaster*, has been found in only a very few places in the short-grass prairie near Cimarron. It is a short-tailed species with a pepper-and-salt pattern dorsally. Though now rare and limited in distribution in our state, at one time the prairie vole occurred as far south-west as Grant County, where its remains have been identified among the bones in a cave deposit dating from the waning phases of the last glacial age. The montane vole, *M. montanus*, has been found only in the Jemez and San Juan mountains, where it is a common inhabitant of montane grasslands. The Pennsylvania vole (*M. pennsylvanicus*) is found in moist habitats in and around the Sangre de Cristo Mountains and in a series of isolated marshes along the San Juan River. Relict colonies that formerly occurred in marshes near Grants and near Aragon, Catron County, have probably become extinct. The two most widespread species are the long-tailed vole, *M. longicaudus*, and the Mexican vole, *M. mexicanus*. The Mexican vole is found in most of the southern and western ranges in the state. It is very short-tailed and brown. The long-tailed vole is found in all the higher and more mesic ranges. It has a relatively long tail, much longer than its hindfoot, and is grayish in color.

OLD WORLD RATS AND MICE

Family Muridae

This family contains over eleven hundred species of small rodents, most of which occur in Old World tropical regions, chiefly in southeast Asia and Africa. Two genera and three or four species have been introduced into the New World as commensals of humans, and some populations have established themselves independently in the wild.

The two New World genera are the rats, genus *Rattus*, and the house mouse, genus *Mus*.

Rattus is one of the most speciose of mammalian genera, with almost six hundred species having been described. The majority are tropical forms native to Asia and Africa. Two subtropical or temperate zone species attached themselves early to humans as commensals and traveled with them to most of the places that people colonized. The first to appear in European records was the black rat, *R. rattus*. This animal seems to have entered Europe with the returning armies of the Crusaders during the period from A.D. 1095 to 1191. Shortly thereafter, it was firmly established on that continent. The black rat was also the first species of the genus to arrive in the New World, and it has been suggested that the first ones may have come with Columbus in 1492. It was well established in the English colonies in North America by the beginning of the eighteenth century. The species spread widely in

North America and was reported from many of the larger cities. In New Mexico, this species has occurred in the lower Rio Grande Valley since at least 1914, and populations persist in the agricultural areas there. Throughout much of the more northern United States, the black rat has become rare or extinct, apparently because of competition from the Norway rat, a more recent immigrant.

The latter species did not arrive in Europe from Central Asia until the early part of the eighteenth century, when it is reported to have moved westward on its own volition, and also to have been introduced by mariners into many of the northern European cities and into Great Britain. *Rattus norvegicus* is believed to have been introduced into North America from England in about the first year of the American Revolution, and to have arrived on the Pacific Coast about 1850. Norway rats have gradually replaced black rats in almost all parts of the United States except the most southern areas, where the latter species is still common. Norway rats were reported to be common in New Mexican towns as early as 1851, probably coming from the east with Anglo immigrants. The animals were reported to be abundant in Albuquerque in 1888. However, in general, this species has had a difficult time in becoming established in the Rocky Mountain region. They are not very common anywhere in New Mexico at the present time.

Members of the genus *Rattus* might be mistaken for a native pack rat of the genus *Neotoma*. However, the introduced animals have a nearly naked, scaly tail (rather than a well-haired, usually bicolored tail), and they are grayish or dark-colored ventrally, rather than white. Black rats are darker in color than Norway rats, and have a tail that is longer than the head and body rather than shorter.

In urban situations both species of *Rattus* live in groups, probably organized in a dominance hierarchy like the groups of house mice. The groups defend foraging areas and tend to exclude strangers, thus limiting the population density. Group members are rather sedentary, seldom having home ranges that exceed one hundred feet in diameter. Where both species occupy the same city, as in San Francisco, some habitat separation is seen. Norway rats live at ground level and in the basements of buildings, while black rats are more common in multi-storied structures. This separation has apparently had an effect on the reproductive cycles of the two: in San Francisco, for example, Norway rats have two breeding peaks, in May and September, seemingly as a result of seasonal weather changes. Black rats are aseasonal breeders, and most live in man-made structures with interior climate control. In parts of the southern United States—in Florida, for example—Norway rats are most common in downtown and commercial areas of cities, while black rats occupy middle-class suburbs and rural sections. Norway rats are burrowers, often living underground, while black rats are climbers. Norway rats are more aggressive and tend to dominate black rats in encounters. Wild-living rats of both species have home ranges of .16 to .25 hectares.

The average litter size is about six babies, born after a twenty-two-day gestation. The young are weaned in about three weeks and become sexually mature at two months of age. Breeding greatly diminishes after eighteen months. Most animals live less than a year.

The laboratory rat is a derivative of *Rattus norvegicus*. Thus, the considerable economic loss that humans suffer because of competition with the Norway rat is at least partially offset by the substantial advances in medicine attributable to the use of the laboratory rat in biomedical research.

Mice of the genus *Mus* are found as natives in Africa and Eurasia. Several species, among the fifteen or so described, have become associated with humans. The wild species, *Mus musculus*, from which the house mouse is derived, is a native of central and southern Asia. It has probably followed human migrations since the beginnings of agriculture, and probably entered North America with the earliest colonists. It has been suggested that the house mouse of the northern United States was derived from the commensal strain of northern Europe and Britain, whereas that of the southern part of the country and of Central and South America stemmed from the domestic populations of the Iberian and Italian peninsulas. House mice are widespread and sometimes rather common in New Mexico. They are quite successful in arid grasslands and in desert areas, which are not unlike the arid central Asian regions of their origins. The mice may live successfully as wild animals, and also enter human habitations, especially in the winter. Throughout the range of the house mouse, commensal populations differ from wild ones in having longer tails and darker coloration, traits which may adapt them to the built environment of man. Most New Mexican specimens seem more typical of wild or feral strains, being paler in color and having shorter tails.

The house mouse might be mistaken for a harvest mouse (*Reithrodontomys*) or a young *Peromyscus* in gray pelage. However, house mice in our area never have white bellies, as do both the native species. Furthermore, *Reithrodontomys* has grooves on the anterior face of the upper incisors, features which are lacking in *Mus*.

Commensal house mice—those living in buildings and farm structures—seem to be organized into small groups within which a dominance hierarchy exists, with the dominant individual being an adult male. The dominant individual does most of the mating of females in the group. The group occupies a defended home area from which casual immigrants are excluded. In these situations, chemical communication between the mice may control their breeding behavior in subtle ways. For example, females reared in association with adult males or with pregnant females may attain puberty earlier (forty-five days) than individuals reared with nonpregnant females (sixty days). Young males reared with adult females mature more quickly than those reared with adult males. The presence of the dominant male in the group may be responsible for the delayed sexual maturation of his sons. If the dominant male disappears, this restraint on the development of other males in the group is removed. If the dominant male disappears and a strange male enters the colony, his presence may cause pregnant females in the group to abort their embryos (the Bruce Effect). Much of this interaction has been shown to be caused by substances in the urine of the mice.

Wild or feral house mice seemingly live rather different social lives. They may not occur in rigidly structured colonies; instead, the individual may have its own home ranges or share a range with one or two others. The ability to disperse rapidly to newly opened and favorable habitats seems to be an important part of the strategy employed by wild mice to maintain their populations. Dispersers in this species are often females in reproductive condition which can quickly expand the immigrant population.

After a twenty-day gestation, female house mice bear from one to twelve or, more commonly, four to five young. As noted, the young attain reproductive maturity in forty-five to sixty days, depending upon the social environment. Laboratory animals may produce fourteen litters annually, but wild mice, which live short lives, may produce only one or two.

While house mice are omnivorous, wild populations feed largely on vegetation (25 percent) and on invertebrates. Commensal animals may kill and eat cockroaches in urban habitats.

JUMPING MICE

Family Zapodidae, Genus *Zapus*

These long-tailed mice with long hind feet might be confused with kangaroo rats. However, the kangaroo rats have a sharply bicolored tail with a long tuft of hairs at the end, hairy soles of the hind feet, and external fur-lined cheek pouches. Jumping mice have terete tails, naked soles, and no external fur-lined cheek pouches. Moreover, kangaroo rats occur in deserts and sandy grasslands. Most jumping mice are found high in the montains. Those that do live in lower elevations are found in the thick grasses and sedges around marshes.

Lush grasses and sedges among willows and alders along cool streams high in the northern mountains are the preferred habitats of jumping mice in New Mexico. Most of the records of occurrence are from the Sangre de Cristo and San Juan mountains, with a few also from the Jemez and Sacramentos. Isolated colonies occur along the Rio Grande at the Bosque del Apache Wildlife Refuge and at the Isleta Marsh, and there are early records for the Rio Grande Valley at Albuquerque and at El Rito.

Individual mice occupy home ranges of .08 to .35 hectares. It is not known if territorial defense occurs, but the animals seem to be solitary most of the time. Late in the summer or early in the fall, the animals enter burrows and become torpid, hibernating until late April or May. *Zapus* is one of the most profound mammalian hibernators, living through the winter period entirely on stored fat. After emergence in the spring, females become pregnant, bearing four to seven young after a gestation of seventeen to eighteen days. The mother may produce a second litter, becoming pregnant while nursing the first babies. Gestation of the second family may extend to twenty-one days. The young are naked and blind. At about four weeks of age they assume adult pelage and slow their growth rate considerably. Weaning has taken place by this time.

Jumping mice prefer the reproductive parts of grasses and dicots, and also eat a variety of insects. There is no evidence that *Zapus* stores food for the winter.

Two species of *Zapus* are found in New Mexico: *Z. princeps*, the western jumping mouse, and *Z. hudsonius*, the meadow jumping mouse. The two are very similar and are distinguished by the study of their teeth and detailed cranial measurements. The western species is exclusively montane in our area. The meadow jumping mouse is found at the Rio Grande Valley stations mentioned earlier and in the Sacramento Mountains.

Porcupine
(Family Erethizontidae)

Erethizon dorsatum.   The porcupine is a mammal well known to most people who spend time in the mountains. The large rodents are most commonly seen sitting in a young pine where the cambial layers of tissue under the bark have provided a meal. Although they are most common in montane forests, "porkies" are found in all habitats through-out the state, occurring in low numbers even in grasslands and deserts. In these lowland situations, the animals seek shelter in caves, rock shelters, or burrows excavated in the sides of arroyos by other animals.

For most people, the distinctive feature of the porcupine is the possession of quills, spiny hairs mixed with the more normal guard hairs of the back and tail. These rigid structures are provided with barbs and are loosely attached so that they easily penetrate and remain with an attacker. Contrary to one belief, porcupines do not throw their quills. However, a threatened animal may lash its tail from side to side with great vigor, and the tail quills may be driven forcibly into the skin of a predator. Nonetheless, a variety of predatory animals have learned to attack and kill porcupines without undue damage to themselves. In Canada, the fisher (*Martes pennanti*) is one of the chief predators. Moun-tain lions also occasionally dine on *Erethizon*. In New Mexico the chief predator of the porcupine is probably man, who kills the animals to prevent them from damaging forest trees. The name *porcupine* is related to a Spanish name for the animals, *puerco espín*, or spiny pig, although the word probably entered English from French or Italian.

Porcupines generally lead solitary lives. Sometimes, several ani-mals may share an especially suitable den, such as a cave or hollow log. Or a pair may spend a period of time together in a feeding tree. Such a tree may be defended against other porcupines. Mating takes place in the fall. Contrary to various fanciful accounts, during copulation the male mounts the female from the rear as is the rule in other rodents. However, copulation is preceded by an elaborate courtship ritual. If fertilization does not occur, the female enters estrus again in 25 to 30 days. Gestation lasts about 210 days. Usually a single young is born fully furred, with its eyes open and its teeth well enough developed so that it can begin eating solid food within the first week of its life. At birth the quills are present but soft, although they harden very quickly and provide the baby with protection. The youngster remains with its mother for several months, but other than nursing, maternal care is not elaborate, and the infant is capable of independent life at an early age. Young females reach sexual maturity at the age of a year and a half. It is not certain how long porcupines live in nature, though there is at least one record of a wild ten-year-old animal.

Porcupines are strict vegetarians. In summer a variety of plants may be consumed, including leaves, berries, roots, flowers, seeds, and water plants. In winter the diet becomes almost exclusively cambium and phloem of various trees. The preferred food tree in our area seems to be the ponderosa pine. An animal may spend a number of days in a single feeding tree, resulting in considerable damage to the tree, especially if the main trunk or branches are girdled. Porcupine damage to pines and other trees is easy to spot in the woods, and provides a means of estimating the abundance of the animals. Because of their winter-feeding habits, porcupines are considered enemies of lumber interests, and are often killed by foresters. However, there is considerable debate about the true extent of loss caused by the animals. Frequently, porcupines seem to prefer younger trees, and their feeding activities often have the effect of thinning dense stands, which would have to be thinned anyway to allow for optimal growth of the remaining trees. The intestine of *Erethizon* contains bacteria which break down cellulose.

The porcupine belongs to a group of rodents most common in the New World and African tropics. For many years, mammalogists have entertained themselves in devising scenarios that might have resulted in this unusual distribution pattern. It is probable that the porcupine or its ancestor entered North America from the south during the early part of the Ice Ages. The earliest known fossil porcupines come from Argentina.

Nutria

Myocastor coypus. The nutria is a large aquatic rodent native to southern South America. It has been introduced into the United States and into many other parts of the world either intentionally or through escapes from fur farms. There have been a few escapes, and at least one intentional introduction, in southern New Mexico.

Nutrias resemble small beavers with round tails. Like beavers and muskrats, they are usually seen in or near the water. They feed upon aquatic vegetation and live in bank burrows or sometimes in houses constructed of water plants. The animals may breed throughout the year. Up to ten young are born after a gestation of 132 days. The babies are very precocial, with open eyes and a full coat of fur. They are able to live independently of the mother after about five days.

The fur of the nutria is useful, and the meat is also sought after. In some areas where they have been introduced, these animals have become serious pests because of damage to irrigation ditches and levees. The destruction of waterfowl habitat has also been attributed to feral populations of nutria.

The word *nutria* means *otter* in Spanish, and is a modification of the Latin *Lutra,* an otter. In South America, the word probably became transferred to the fur of *Myocaster,* which bears some resemblance to that of South American otters. In South America local names, other than nutria, are often applied to the animal, such as coypu, which is sometimes used as an English common name. The Rio Nutria in the Zuñi Mountains was undoubtedly named after *Lutra,* not *Myocaster.*

Carnivorous Mammals

ORDER CARNIVORA

Mammals of the order Carnivora are characterized by a large number of teeth, most prominently two upper and two lower canine or stabbing teeth, which are more or less conical in form, and often a specialized set of shearing teeth, the carnassial pair, consisting of the upper fourth premolar and the lower first molar. The dentition of carnivores thus functions chiefly to kill and to hold prey, and then to slice up skin and muscle. Some carnivores have become modified for an omnivorous diet; in such cases, the shearing function of the carnassial teeth is diminished, as in bears and raccoons. Characteristically, the brains of carnivores are relatively larger than those of most of their prey animals. Carnivores such as bears, raccoons, and weasels walk on the soles of their feet (plantigrade), or as in the case of dogs and cats, they may be specialized for running and for walking on their toes (digitigrade). Because most carnivores are near or at the top of the energy pyramids in their ecosystems, they tend to be rare.

The twenty-five kinds of carnivores known to inhabit New Mexico now or in the past constitute five families, There are six dogs, two bears, three raccoons, eleven weasels, and three cats.

Bears look like huge, lumbering dogs without tails. Members of the raccoon family all have long tails with dark and light rings around them. All of the cats look like larger versions of the house cat, except that the bobcat has a short stubby tail. Members of the dog family look more or less like domestic dogs, and all have a long bushy tail. That leaves the weasel family, which contains a diverse assemblage including skunks, true weasels, badgers, and otters. The smallest of all these carnivores is the ermine, which is small enough to fit into the runway of a meadow vole; and the largest is the grizzly bear, which may exceed fifteen hundred pounds. Carnivores have thus diversified to take advantage of prey animals from mice to the largest ungulates.

WOLVES, COYOTES, AND FOXES

Family Canidae

Among carnivores, canids are the most specialized for cursorial (running) locomotion. Their legs are relatively long, especially the foot segment, and they stand on the bottoms of their toes (a digitigrade posture). Members of the family are further distinguished externally by a long bushy tail, an elongate muzzle, and rather large pointed ears.

Six members of the dog family either now live in New Mexico, or have lived here within this century. One species, the gray wolf, *Canis lupus*, has been extinct in the area since the late 1940s or early 1950s. Most commonly seen is the coyote, *C. latrans*, which has a black tailtip and is about the size of a small German shepherd. The gray fox also has a black-tipped tail, but in addition, it has a black stripe down the top of the tail; it is usually confined to rocky or wooded areas, while the coyote is often seen in open deserts and grasslands. The kit and swift foxes have black-tipped tails as well, but they are much smaller, perhaps the size of a large house cat. Coyotes are often seen in the daytime, while a diurnal sighting is rare for a kit or swift fox.

COYOTE

Canis latrans

The coyote is widely distributed in New Mexico, and may be seen in almost every life zone and habitat from alpine meadows down to desert. Despite control programs aimed at reducing their numbers, they are relatively common. In some of the more densely settled parts of the central United States, coyotes are, if anything, more common than they were when Europeans first entered the region.

Coyotes are less social than wolves or domestic dogs, but more so than foxes. The animals often hunt alone, or a mated pair may cooperate in foraging. Pairings are monogamous and may last for several years, though not necessarily for the life of the coyote. A courtship of several months precedes attempts at copulation. The females are monestrous, coming into heat once a year, usually in the late winter or early spring. Heat lasts from two to five days. As in the wolf and domestic dog, the copulating pair are locked together for a period of up to a half-hour. Gestation lasts approximately sixty-three days. An average of six pups is delivered in a burrow constructed by the adult in a hollow log, in the burrow of another animal, or in a natural shelter. Rarely, two females may share the same burrow. The babies are weaned between the fifth and seventh week, but they begin to eat solid food at about the third week. The mother, and possibly the father, regurgitate partially digested food for the growing pups. The young begin to emerge from the den at about two to three weeks of age, and disperse after six to nine months. Some young may remain with the mother and father, and for a time a small group is formed. Probably, the group is organized in a dominance hierarchy. Yearling males and females are capable of breeding, but most probably wait until their second year of life. The maximum age in the wild is probably six to eight years.

Although about 90 percent of the coyote's diet is mammalian flesh, they are opportunistic, and depending upon season and availability, consume a wide variety of plant and animal material. In some areas in the Southwest, jackrabbits are a favored item. During the winter in western rangelands, a high proportion of the diet is the carrion of larger game and domestic animals. Although coyotes do prey upon livestock, most of the individuals actually killed are young or infirm individuals. Debate over the importance of coyotes as threats to ranching and farming interests has rarely provided solutions. Extensive control programs have been carried out, especially in the West; but it has never been demonstrated that coyotes limit game or livestock populations, and it is not clear that the cost of control is justified in many cases. The rancher who loses animals to coyote predation is certainly justified in seeking to control his losses. Often, however, the cause of death of a domestic animal is not known with certainty.

Gray Wolf

Canis lupus.   Despite a variety of common names, such as timber wolf, lobo, prairie wolf, and the like, there are only two known species of wolves in the world: the present species, which ranged through most of North America and across Europe and Asia, and the red wolf, *C. rufus,* which formerly inhabited the southeastern United States. Like most other widespread animals and plants, the gray wolf shows a fair amount of geographic variation in size and color, leading to the use of regional common names. Until early in the twentieth century, wolves were common throughout the West, including New Mexico. The normal prey of the gray wolf is medium-sized and large mammals, principally deer and other ungulates. This predilection brought the wolf into direct competition with human interests, and led to early and vigorous attempts to eliminate the wolf from western rangelands. During the last century, wolves were abundant in New Mexico. By 1917 it was estimated that 103 remained in the state; by 1918, 45; and by 1939, 30. Shortly thereafter, the few remaining New Mexican lobos were those whose hunting route took them through the southern part of Hidalgo County and back into Chihuahua and Sonora. Probably even these wanderers failed to appear by the end of the 1940s. Today no wolves are left in the western United States, except for a possibly reestablished population in Idaho, Montana, and Wyoming. The Mexican population is probably nearing extinction. Nonetheless, there are persistent reports of wolf sightings in various mountain regions of New Mexico. In all likelihood, these sightings all pertain to domestic dogs or coyotes, or perhaps to dog–coyote hybrids.

Wolves are the most social among the North American members of the dog family. A typical social unit is a family consisting of an adult pair and their pups. In such a group, the male is dominant, the female is number two, and the pups have a dominance order among themselves. After a courtship of varying duration, copulation takes place during the female's five- to seven-day heat. After a sixty-three-day gestation, an average of six blind and helpless young are born, usually in an underground burrow. The mother remains with the pups for about two months, during which time the male and other pack members may bring food for mother and her babies. The young wolves reach adult size in a year, but often they do not breed until they are three years of age. Ten years is the approximate life span of wild wolves.

Wolves prey chiefly on larger hooved mammals such as deer, elk, moose, caribou, bison, and mountain sheep. The hunting of such prey requires a group effort in which the pack participates. Studies of wolf predation on moose show that only a small percentage of their attacks are successful. In areas where deer are a principal prey, it has been estimated that the average predation rate is about one deer per wolf every eighteen days.

It is probable that the chief ancestor of the domestic dog is *Canis lupus*. The tendency of wolf pups to socialize strongly, to integrate into group life, and to accept the leadership role of dominant individuals suits them to life with groups of humans. Many of the behaviors that dogs display toward their human dominants are the same ones shown toward dominant individuals of their own species. Wolves and dogs hybridize readily, seemingly without loss of fertility in the offspring. Dogs and coyotes hybridize as well, but the offspring are not fully fertile. Under certain conditions, domestic dogs become feral and form small hunting groups, which are organized somewhat like wolf packs. Such feral dogs, once adjusted to life in the wild, greatly reduce their tendency to engage in the neurotic barking of their civilized relatives. A few wild dogs may exist in certain mountain areas in New Mexico, and may provide the basis for some wolf reports.

Red Fox

Vulpes vulpes. The red fox is distinctive among New Mexican members of the dog family in having a white-tipped tail. In our region, it is chiefly a montane species, with most state records coming from the Sangre de Cristo and San Juan mountains. There are a few reports from Doña Ana County, a few from the San Juan Valley, and two from the east side of the state. In Colorado the species is also chiefly found in the mountains, with a very few records from the plains. Some evidence suggests that eastern red foxes have been moving westward into the plains regions since about 1920. It is not clear if our records from the east side pertain to mountain individuals that have moved into the lowlands or to immigrants from the east.

Red foxes generally prefer areas with a reasonable amount of rainfall and vegetation. Good rodent populations probably play a part in making an area suitable. Foxes form monogamous pairs. Mating takes place in spring, and from four to ten young are born after a fifty-one-day gestation. The young remain in their natal shelter, usually an underground burrow, for about five weeks, and they become independent at about five months of age. During the period of dependency, both the mother and the babies are partially supplied with food by the father.

Small rodents, especially various mice, such as *Microtus*, form a staple for these foxes. In agricultural areas foxes are probably a net asset to farmers, although the poultry farmer might on occasion disagree with that assessment. The fur is quite valuable, and red foxes have formed the basis for a profitable fur-ranching industry for many years. Because of their rarity in New Mexico, they are of little economic importance here.

KIT AND SWIFT FOXES

Vulpes macrotis and *V. velox*

These little desert foxes resemble each other closely, and mammalogists have sometimes concluded that they were actually members of the same species. However, where the geographic ranges of the two meet in southeastern New Mexico, there is no gradation in characteristics from one to the other, but rather a very narrow zone of contact in which a few hybrids are found. On this basis, most students prefer to regard the two as distinct kinds. Nonetheless, the known habits of the two species are much the same. The eastern species, the swift fox, *Vulpes velox*, has shorter ears, a broader head, and a shorter tail than its western relative the kit fox, *V. macrotis*.

Throughout New Mexico, desert foxes live in open country, deserts, and grasslands. They live in burrows, probably those that they dig themselves. Like red foxes, they tend to live as monogamous pairs, although instances of trios—a male and two females—have been reported. Females select natal dens in the fall, and males join them at that time. Mating takes place from December through February. The pair stays together through at least one season, and monogamy for life has been suggested. The length of gestation is unknown, but it is estimated to be from forty-nine to fifty-six days. A litter of four to five pups is born in February or March. While the babies are being nursed the female rarely leaves the den, and the male seems to be responsible for most of the provisioning. Later, both parents bring food to the pups. Regurgitation of food by the parents has not been reported; instead, whole prey animals are offered to the young. Pups reach adult size at about five months of age. The families separate in the fall. Young females do not reproduce until their second year.

Desert foxes seem to be opportunistic carnivores, often feeding on the most common rodents or lagomorphs in the area. Some studies have revealed a diet almost entirely composed of kangaroo rats, while other investigators have reported large numbers of black-tailed jackrabbits in the menu. Birds, small reptiles, and insects are also eaten.

Densities of foxes vary with the productivity of the habitat for their prey and with the extent of human predation. Estimates of the range of a pair of kit foxes are from five hundred to one thousand acres. Natural predators probably include the coyote, but there are few accounts of predation of any sort.

Gray Fox

Urocyon cinereoargenteus.   The gray fox is readily distinguished from other New Mexican foxes by the black ridge of hair running down the top of the tail, and the black tailtip. The dorsal pelage is grizzled gray.

This is an animal of broken country and woodlands. Grays are uncommon or absent in grasslands and deserts unless rocky areas are present, and the species also seems to be rare in mixed coniferous and spruce-fir forests. However, since woodland and rocks are a dominant feature of the New Mexican landscape, these attractive foxes are also widespread and quite common in the state.

Urocyon is thought to live in family units consisting of a pair of adults and their pups. Some evidence suggests that these families maintain territories, but other studies indicate that home ranges of family units may be widely overlapping. As with other foxes, it has been suggested that grays are monogamous, but data to support this contention are derived chiefly from anecdotes. Breeding takes place in late winter and early spring. The gestation period is not known, but estimates of fifty-three to sixty-three days have been published. One to seven young have been reported, but the most common litter size is four. Young animals may follow the mother on foraging trips at three months, becoming independent at four months of age. The foxes live several years in the wild, and maximum ages of individuals in nature are around fourteen to fifteen years. Estimates of density range from one to two per square kilometer.

Gray foxes are quite omnivorous. In certain seasons small mammals form the chief staple, but during late summer a variety of plants are consumed. Juniper berries and piñon nuts fill many gray fox scats collected in woodland areas, and squawbush (*Rhus trilobata*) is also a common food. These animals are quite adept at climbing, and are frequently seen far above the ground in large cottonwoods, oaks, and piñons.

Black Bear

Ursus americanus.   Grizzly bears are presumed to be extinct in New Mexico; thus, any sighting of a bear in our state is undoubtedly of a black bear. Nonetheless, the persistent reports of grizzly sightings in the San

Juan Mountains, adjacent to northwestern New Mexico in Colorado, makes the possibility of seeing a grizzly in that area somewhat more than zero. Grizzlies are best distinguished from black bears by the very high shoulder region of the former, much higher than any other areas of the back. Grizzlies often move with their heads held high, somewhat like a dog. Black bears, in contrast, have shoulders that are about the same height as the rest of the back, or even lower, and the head is usually held lower than the rest of the body. Grizzlies move with an alert doglike trot or brisk walk. Black bears shamble along, almost as though they were stiff and sore, certainly not in a hurry.

Black bears are still found in most of the forested parts of New Mexico, and it is not uncommon to find them around mountain campgrounds, and even fairly near to large population centers. The bears tend to be solitary foragers, usually setting forth in the evening and roaming over several miles before morning. During the day, shelter is sought in a resting place among boulders or logs. These are highly omnivorous animals. Almost any kind of food is acceptable. In season, various fruits and other plant products are consumed; a great deal of time is spent in looking for invertebrates and small vertebrates; and occasionally, larger animals are taken. At various places in the home range of a bear are trees from which the animals have scratched the bark, leaving many claw marks. These bear trees, together with characteristic large scats often packed with the remains of seeds, are good indications of a bear's local presence.

Bears mate in June or July. However, the embryos do not implant themselves in the uterine wall of the mother until perhaps November, remaining dormant in the uterus in the form of a tiny ball of cells. The babies are born about the end of January. Thus, the time from copulation to birth is about seven months; however, the embryos have been growing in the uterus for only about two months. When the two or three babies are born, the mother is in hibernation. The young are very tiny, perhaps six to eight inches long; they are sparsely haired, and have their eyes closed. The eyes open in about five weeks, and when the young first leave the den, in March or April, they may weigh from six to eight pounds apiece. The cubs remain with their mother during their first winter, and disperse the following spring. Puberty is not reached until the young animals are about four years old. The females produce a litter every other year. Wild bears may occasionally live as long as twenty-five years.

In winter, bears retreat to a den and go into a deep sleep. They do not truly hibernate because the body temperature does not drop to very low levels; little lower, in fact, that the normal operating temperature. Bears may arouse from this sleep fairly readily, and occasionally they awake and make short trips outside.

Grizzly Bear

Ursus arctos.   Unlike black bears, grizzlies were common in open grasslands as well as in forested areas. The grizzly is essentially like the black in most aspects of natural history, including promiscuous mating behavior, delayed implantation of embryos, winter sleep, and omnivory. Because of its larger size, the grizzly is capable of killing large animals, and probably does so more frequently than their black relatives. Reports of grizzlies killing cattle and horses were common in the early days in the West. For the most part, however, those large mammals that were fed upon by grizzlies probably entered their diet in the form of carrion. The last grizzly bear in New Mexico was probably killed in the 1930s.

Raccoon

Procyon lotor.   The raccoon is readily recognized as an animal the size of a large cat, possessing a ringed tail, a pointed and foxlike muzzle, and a black mask across the eyes. The ring-tailed cat, *Bassariscus,* also has a ringed tail, but the animal is smaller and slighter of build, lacks a black facial mask, and instead, has two prominent white eye-rings. The coatimundi, *Nasua,* has a very long ringed tail, but lacks the distinct black mask and has partial eye-rings as well as a very long slender snout; it is likely to be seen only in the extreme southwestern part of the state.

Raccoons are widespread in New Mexico, and are usually found in the vicinity of watercourses or in wooded and forested areas. They are sometimes seen, however, in deserts and grasslands far from permanent water. They may be more common now than they were early in the century, when the first wide-ranging surveys were made.

Raccoons are solitary, except during the period when the young accompany their mother. Individuals shelter in caves, in burrows, or by preference, in hollow trees. During the colder part of the winter, several individuals may occupy a single den and enter a profound sleep without, however, entering hibernation with its attendant lowered body temperature. In late winter, males become sexually active and seek out receptive females. A single male may mate with several females. Gestation takes from sixty-three to sixty-five days, and the three or four young are born in early spring. The newborns are very sparsely furred and blind. They first leave the den at about two months of age and follow the mother on her foraging trips. Frequently, the youngsters spend their first winter in a den with their mother. Some of the young may become sexually active in their first year, but most do not enter the breeding population in a functional sense until their second year of life. Home ranges of adults vary considerably in size, up to three kilometers in diameter, and overlap broadly, with no demonstration of territorial defense.

Raccoons tend to forage at night, and are quite omnivorous in their diets. Seasonally, they may consume large quantities of fruits and grains. Aquatic animals, such as crayfish and frogs, are favored items; and a variety of other small animals, vertebrate as well as invertebrate, are accepted. The specific epithet of the raccoon, *lotor,* means "the washer," and refers to the habit of captive raccoons of putting their food in water and manipulating it with their hands. Wild raccoons have never been observed in doing this, and it has been suggested that the captives behave as they do because they normally capture much of their food in water. In any event, the function seems not to be the cleansing of the food.

Ringtail

Bassariscus astutus.   Ringtails are inhabitants of rocky or broken country from the desert into the lower forest zones. They are widespread in New Mexico, and probably rather common, although they are seldom seen. Their predilection for rocky areas is coupled with adaptations for climbing in difficult situations. They are known to use chimney-climbing techniques in moving through narrow crevices, to rotate front and hind feet outward to enable them to traverse narrow edges, and to reverse direction on narrow ledges, to utilize accurate power jumping, and to employ a richochetal path to jump to places difficult to reach. Additional anatomical adaptations for climing include partially retractile claws on all four feet.

Little is known of the social life of ringtails. Groups are known to appear together at feeding stations, and the foraging area of an individual has been determined as 140 hectares.

Females den in rocky areas. Three or four young are born in May and June. Seemingly, the male helps in provisioning the family. The young begin foraging with the parents at two months of age, and are nearly adult size at four and a half months.

Like other procyonids, ringtails are omnivorous. Some studies have shown that a great deal of plant material is consumed, but most of the evidence is that these animals are more carnivorous than the raccoon, consuming many birds, small mammals, and small reptiles. Carrion of larger mammals is regularly consumed, and as a result, many scats contain remains of deer and cattle. Foraging takes place chiefly at night.

Coatimundi

Nasua nasua.   The coatimundi is a widespread inhabitant of tropical and warm temperature areas in Mexico and in Central and South America; it barely enters the United States in southern Texas, New Mexico, and Arizona. The only verified records for our state are from the Animas and Peloncillo mountains of extreme southern Hidalgo County, the Gila Valley, the Burro Mountains in Grant County, and the San Francisco drainage in Catron County.

Coatis are much more social than other members of the raccoon family. Females and their young may remain together for a time after the young become independent, and join other such families, resulting in the formation of a rather large troop whose members then stay together for foraging. Males are not warmly welcomed into the troop, and when they are allowed to join they are dominated by the adult females. Such males mate with those females that become receptive, but otherwise no pair bond seems to be formed. Pregnant females leave the group while they have their young. The gestation is approximately seventy-one to seventy-seven days. The young may be born in spring, but the timing of parturition may vary depending on local circumstances. For example, in Central American tropical forests, the young emerge from the nest at a time when falling fruit provides an easy living. After the young leave at about five weeks of age, the family then may rejoin a troop. At about this time, the males leave the troops and take up a solitary existence.

Like other procyonids, coatis are omnivores. In areas where it is plentiful, fruit forms a staple. In other seasons or places, invertebrates and small vertebrates provide an important part of the diet. Single males may spend considerable time in hunting for small rodents. Coatis can climb well, and sometimes forage in the trees. In southern Arizona, it has been suggested that ground-dwelling birds and their nests frequently fall victim to the coatis, but evidence is scanty.

WEASELS, OTTERS, BADGERS, AND SKUNKS

Family Mustelidae

At first glance, the inclusion of these diverse carnivores in a single family might seem unreasonable. Indeed, these animals differ considerably in morphology and behavior. They are linked by the common possession of various cranial features, and all possess anal scent glands. Each group tends to specialize in a different way of making a living. Weasels are efficient predators of small vertebrates. Otters exploit aquatic prey. Badgers are specialists in excavating rodents and other burrowing prey in deserts and grasslands. Skunks are preeminent omnivores.

WEASELS

Mustela and *Martes*

Weasels are short-legged, elongate, tubular carnivores with short faces and quick movements. All are highly carnivorous, and are efficient killers of small vertebrates. The marten, *Martes*, differs from the other weasels because it is highly arboreal and uniformly golden brown except for the throat region, which is orange. The other weasels are terrestrial or aquatic, and not colored as described.

Pine Marten

Martes americana.   Pine martens are inhabitants of the transcontinental coniferous forest, reaching New Mexico only in the high northern mountains. There, a few exist in the spruce-fir forest and in the timberline areas.

Martens live solitary lives during most of the year. Males have large foraging areas that may encompass the ranges of several females. The home range of a male may cover a square mile, while that of a female is about a quarter of that size. Females become receptive in summer, and the two sexes consort briefly during the period in which mating takes place. After a brief period of development, to about the blastocyst stage when it is a solid ball of cells, the embryo ceases active cell division and remains unimplanted in the uterus until about February or March. After a period of twenty-five to twenty-eight days of further development, the two to five babies are born, usually in March or April. The young are weaned at six to seven weeks of age, and are nearly adult size in six to seven months.

Prey consists of small vertebrates, probably mostly mammals. Because of their climbing ability, martens are able to pursue and capture arboreal prey, and the red squirrel, *Tamiasciurus,* is a favored item.

The fur of *Martes* is especially thick and soft, and it has been an important commercial item in the past. Because of their rarity in our region, the animals are of no economic importance.

Ermine

Mustela erminea.   These small weasels are two-toned, brown above and white below, and have a black tailtip. They resemble the long-tailed weasel, *M. frenata,* but in New Mexico the latter's underparts are suffused with orange, and frequently it has a facial mask of black and white. Ermines occasionally have a yellowish ventral wash, but are never orange in that region.

This species is found in northern regions around the world. They are found in the higher mountains of the northern part of New Mexico, with the southernmost record coming from the Sandías. Ermines live on the edges of forests, in meadows, and in rocky areas in the forested zones. Their small size allows them to enter the burrows of small rodents, especially voles, which are one of their dietary staples. Specimens are sometimes taken in live traps set in vole runways. Males are substantially larger (40 to 80 percent in weight) than females. It has been suggested that this difference leads to a difference in the size of prey selected, thereby reducing intraspecific competition. However, it seems more likely that social structure is an important driving force in maintaining the dimorphism. Males cover larger territories that include the home ranges of several females. Larger males are presumably able to encompass the ranges of more females as well as defend more successfully this area against other males.

Males and females may form a brief pair bond while the female is in heat during late spring and summer. At this time, the female is rearing young resulting from the previous year's mating, and the male may offer some help in caring for the babies. The six to nine young are weaned by about the fifth week. The attending male may copulate with the young females during their time in the nest, possibly before their eyes are open. Both the adult female and her inseminated daughters carry the unimplanted blastocysts until the following March or April, when they bear the young after a three- to four-week gestation.

The food of ermines is chiefly small rodents, rabbits, and birds. When these items are in short supply, other small animals are consumed. The density of ermines, however, seems dependent on the density of rodents and lagomorphs. In our area, where the ermine coexists with the larger long-tailed weasel, *erminea* probably concentrates on smaller prey.

Ermines have two molts per year, one in the spring and one in the fall. In northern parts of their range, after the fall molt the animals grow a white coat, except for the black tailtip, and in the spring they change to brown again. In more southern areas the winter pelage is also brown. The difference seems to be genetic, since ermines from winter-white regions continue to turn white when moved to more southern latitudes, and their offspring for several generations persist in molting to a white winter pelage. Initiation of molt is caused by decreasing daylength; however, the actual shedding of fur in spring is retarded by low temperatures. Therefore, in long winters the white coat is not shed at an inappropriately early date. Production of brown hairs is mediated by a hormone, the elaboration of which is inhibited by low temperatures.

Long-Tailed Weasel

Mustela frenata.   This species is distinguished from the ermine as described previously. In our area, there is a real chance of mistaking the long-tailed weasel for a black-footed ferret, *M. nigripes,* a rare inhabitant of prairie dog towns. Long-tailed weasels from lowland areas and from the southern part of the state have facial masks, dark areas around the eyes set off from the surrounding brown fur by white hair. In this feature, they closely resemble the ferret. Unlike the ferret, however, *M. frenata* lacks black feet, and is sharply bicolored. The ferret has black feet and is only weakly, if at all, bicolored. This should make identification easy. Nonetheless, long-tailed weasels inhabit prairie dog towns, and are sometimes seen peering from the burrows in such a way that the feet cannot be seen. Montane *frenata* lack the mask.

This species is widespread in New Mexico and occurs in most available habitats where suitable prey is found. Because of its larger size, *frenata* preys upon slightly larger animals than does *erminea,* taking ground squirrels and rabbits more frequently than mice. Like the ermine, the long-tailed weasel pursues a variety of other prey when necessary.

Social organization of the long-tailed weasel is probably somewhat like that of the ermine. Individuals lead solitary lives during most of the year. Males and females consort during midsummer, and copulation takes place at that time. Males may also mate with the young females, about three months old. Delayed implantation results in cessation of embryonic growth until the blastocyst implants in the uterine wall of the female in late winter. Actual time from implantation to birth of the four to nine young is twenty-three to twenty-four days. The young are weaned at five weeks and reach full size at ten to eleven weeks of age.

Long-tailed weasels turn white in winter in the northern parts of their range, but they stay brown year-round in more southern regions. In New Mexico, the animals turn white at least as far south as Mount Taylor.

Black-Footed Ferret

Mustela nigripes.   The distinguishing features of this large weasel are the black facial mask and the black feet (see account of *M. frenata*).

The black-footed ferret is seemingly an obligate inhabitant of prairie dog towns. Massive changes throughout the former range of the prairie dog, associated with the development of agricultural and grazing indus- tries by humans, have resulted in the reduction of the number and extent of dog towns to the point where few of them are extensive enough to support ferrets. The result is that the ferret has become one of the rarer small mammals in North America, persisting in only a few parts of its former range. There are few actual records of black-footed ferrets in New Mexico, but they indicate a former range in the lowlands of the central part of the state. No verified records have been received in recent years. However, the noctural and very secretive habits of the animal make it unlikely that any but the most careful observer would see them even if they were present.

Little is known of the habits of *nigripes*. The animals may be ter- ritorial. Mating takes place in March and April. There seems to be no, or at least only a brief, period of delayed implantation. Recorded time from copulation to birth is forty-two or forty-five days. The young leave the burrow at about two months of age. Males are about 10 percent larger than females; sexual dimorphism is thus not so pronounced as in the ermine and long-tailed weasel. This phenomenon, as well as the fact that prolonged delay in implantation is not seen, suggest a rather different social strategy than that employed by other weasels.

Ferrets feed primarily on prairie dogs and ground squirrels, but other small to medium-sized mammals are also captured.

Mink

Mustela vison.   Mink are distinguished from other weasels by their rich dark-brown coloration. Some individuals may have a small white area on the throat, but the throat is never golden as in the marten, and mink are never bicolored like the ermine and long-tailed weasel, or masked like the ferret.

This is the most aquatic of the species of *Mustela.* Their preferred habitat is in the vicinity of permanent bodies of water. In our state the few records come from northern areas, the northern mountains, and the San Juan Valley. The southernmost record is from the vicinity of Los Lunas.

Like other *Mustela,* minks are solitary except during the mating season, which lasts from about January through March. At that time, the male and female may share a burrow. Three to six young are born in April or May, after forty to seventy-five days of apparent gestation. The variation seems to be caused by variation in the length of the delay in implantation, and the actual period of embryonic development is about thirty days. The young are weaned at five to six weeks, and hunt with the female at about eight weeks. Females mature sexually at the age of ten months.

Much of the mink's hunting effort is carried out in the water. A variety of aquatic animals is consumed. Crayfish may make up an important part of the diet, and muskrats are common prey. Minks can swim well under water, and are agile enough to capture fish.

As with other weasels, the fur of *M. vison* has considerable commercial appeal. Much of the mink fur used is from animals raised in commercial ranches. Because of their rarity, mink are not of much economic importance in New Mexico.

Badger

Taxidea taxus.   Badgers are readily recognized by their large size (up to twenty pounds), short legs, grizzled gray body, and white facial stripe running along the dorsal midline of the head and across the neck. No other New Mexican mammal possesses this appearance.

Badgers inhabit all open country in New Mexico from the desert up to alpine meadows. Their presence and abundance are closely tied to the local abundance of burrowing rodents, such as prairie dogs, ground squirrels, and pocket gophers. While badgers are not commonly seen, their presence may be detected by the characteristic signs of their burrowings in pursuit of rodent prey.

As with other members of the weasel family, badgers are solitary except for a brief time during the mating season which takes place in August and September. Implantation of the embryo is delayed until about January, and the one to five young are born in an underground burrow in April or May. Males are not involved in caring for the babies. The youngsters are weaned at two months, and they leave the family late in the summer or fall. Young females normally do not breed until their second year of life.

Adult badgers range widely (up to two square miles) in search of prey. The animals are powerful and rapid diggers, easily capable of excavating most burrowing rodents. It has been estimated that consumption of about 1.7 pocket gophers per day is enough to keep a badger going. Mice, insects, and small reptiles, as well as a few birds, have been recorded in the diet. Carrion is sometimes consumed as well. An adult badger is a formidable opponent for a dog, or even for an unarmed human, and it is probably immune to most predation.

SKUNKS

Spilogale, Mephitis, Conepatus

Skunks are alike in their striking black-and-white pattern and in the use of their anal scent glands as defensive weapons. While all members of the weasel family have the glands, and indeed are able to secrete a powerful scent, skunks are outstanding in the degree to which they have perfected the ability to spray the scent at an attacker.

Four species of skunks inhabit New Mexico. The spotted skunk, *Spilogale*, displays a pattern of spots and stripes, and is the smallest of the four. The hog-nosed skunk, *Conepatus*, has a single broad white stripe that covers the entire back and tail, and the snout is naked dorsally, specialized for rooting in the soil. Striped skunks, *Mephitis*, are quite variable in color pattern, but they are never colored like the spotted or hog-nosed species. The common striped skunk, *M. mephitis*, usually has a dorsal white stripe that divides into a V in back of the head. It is an abundant species found all over the state. The hooded skunk, *M. macroura*, rarely has the V-shaped stripe. The back may be entirely white or entirely black with white lateral stripes. The tail of *macroura* is noticeably longer than that of *mephitis*. The hooded skunk is rare, and is found only in Catron, Grant, and Hidalgo counties.

Spotted Skunk

Spilogale putorius.   These animals inhabit rocky and brushy areas in woodlands, grasslands, and deserts. They are widespread in New

Mexico, and seem to be more common in the western part of the state. Because they are seldom seen, they appear to be uncommon, but studies of their abundance are lacking.

Individuals seem to be solitary except during the September mating season, and perhaps during the winter, when several animals may share a den. Adult females as well as those born earlier in the year are all inseminated during the fall. Implantation of the embryo is delayed for 180 to 200 days, and is followed by a 30-day period of development. The young are born in April or May, with litter size ranging from four to nine. The young are weaned at eight weeks, and are full grown at twelve to thirteen weeks of age. Males are larger than females, and are promiscuous in their mating habits.

Spilogales are omnivores, but they have a strong preference for insects and small rodents. Plant products are consumed in season, but insects probably predominate in the diet when they are available. The skunks are much more agile than the other species and are able to climb well, which gives them the option of preying upon birds.

Like the other skunks, *Spilogale* defends itself by spraying scent at predators. In its warning posture, it may stand on its front feet and raise its entire body vertically.

STRIPED SKUNKS

Mephitis

By far the most common, or at least the most commonly seen skunk in our area is the common striped skunk, *M. mephitis*. These animals are found at all elevations and in all life zones. They are commonly observed as road kills, perhaps in part because they are rather slow and deliberate in their movement, and in part because they may find it hard to believe that the automobile will have the temerity to attack them.

Striped skunks are solitary wanderers, and seem not to be territorial since their home ranges overlap widely. They may share communal winter dens, and the young may consort with the mother for a period after they have left the nest. Skunks seem to be promiscuous in their mating habits. Breeding takes place in February or March. Gestation is recorded as sixty-three days after copulation, but it is not recorded if there is a delay in implantation. Four to eleven young are born in April or May and weaned at about six to eight weeks, at which time they begin to follow the female on foraging trips.

Skunks are very omnivorous, consuming insects, small vertebrates, and plant material. Their foraging tactics involve a good deal of shallow digging with their well-developed front claws, and they also search under stones, branches, leaves, and other shelters for small animals.

Not unexpectedly, skunks have rather few serious predators. However, some animals do seem willing to tolerate their chemical defenses. Among these are horned owls (*Bubo*), which seemingly pick up skunks on a regular basis. Domestic dogs often seem undeterred, repeatedly attacking and sometimes killing skunks. It has been suggested that if one picks up a skunk by the tail one can avoid being sprayed, but few people have actually tested this recommendation. Pet skunks tend not to spray their friends, but they may forget themselves in the presence of strange dogs. Skunks can be descented, but the animals then become entirely helpless in the face of threats and cannot be returned to the wild. Rabies is fairly common in skunks, and it is wise for humans to avoid contact with free-living animals.

The hooded skunk has not been studied with respect to its natural history. It seems to be more restricted to the vicinity of watercourses than *M. mephitis*. Nothing is known of its social or reproductive life. It has been reported to bring forth five young in May or June.

Hog-Nosed Skunk

Conepatus mesoleucus.   This is an animal of warmer southern parts of the state, where it has been observed from the creosote desert to the lower pine forests of the southern mountain ranges. There is a 1902 record for the Sandía Mountains, but none has come to the attention of naturalists in that area during the intervening years.

These skunks mate in February or March, and after a two-month gestation they bring forth two to three young. By August, the young are able to pursue independent lives. Nothing is known of the social lives of these animals.

In Texas *Conepatus* is known as the rooter skunk because of its habit of plowing up the ground with its nose and claws in its search for buried small animals, chiefly insects. This rooting behavior leaves unmistakable evidence of the presence of the animals in the area.

Otter

Lutra candensis.   Otters are large (ten to twenty pounds), weasel-like, brown animals with webbed feet and a tapering tail, which is almost the diameter of the body at the base. They are usually seen in or near the water.

They are the most specialized for aquatic life of all western members of the weasel family except for the sea otter, *Enhydra*. River otters are largely limited to the vicinity of larger permanent bodies of water. The only specimen preserved from New Mexico was captured on the Gila River, near Cliff, in 1954. While there are old sight records for the upper Rio Grande and the Canadian valleys, the species has probably never been common in the state; it is certainly extremely rare, if not extinct, within our borders now.

Otters have a social pattern like that of the weasels. The male has a large territory which he may mark and defend against other males, especially during the mating season. Within this area there may be the smaller territories of several females. Mating takes place in March or April, while the females are nursing their litters. The blastocyst remains unimplanted until the following January or February. After implantation, approximately two months elapse until the one to four young are born. The young grow rapidly, and leave the den at about six weeks of age. Male otters have been reported to assume some paternal behavior when the young are partly grown.

Otters are very carnivorous, and find most of their food in the water. Fish, frogs, and turtles are among the vertebrates on the menu, and crayfish are an important part of the diet.

CATS

Family Felidae

Three native cats occur, or have occurred in New Mexico within historic time. The jaguar and the puma are very large and have long tails. The bobcat is of medium size and has a very short tail. The jaguar is spotted, and the puma is not. Only the puma and bobcat are likely to be seen in New Mexico.

Jaguar

Felis onca. Jaguars are typically inhabitants of tropical lowlands, occurring as far north in western Mexico as central Sonora. From 1900 to 1904 a number of jaguars were seen or killed in New Mexico, mostly in the western part of the state, although there is a record from Santa Fe and another from Springer. In Arizona there are records from 1912 to 1949. It is not certain if these records pertain to wanderers from Mexico, or if there was formerly a resident population of jaguars in the southwestern mountains. The likelihood of seeing one in our area is quite low.

Mexican jaguars mate in December and January, and bear two to four young after a gestation of 93 to 110 days. The male and female form a pair bond which lasts through the season of parenthood. The young animals follow the parents at six weeks of age, and disperse at one year. Adults are said to require a foraging area of one hundred to two hundred square miles.

Food consists of large vertebrates, chiefly deer and javelina. Jaguars are somewhat aquatic, enjoy swimming, and sometimes capture and consume fish. The word *jaguar* is of Amazonian Indian origin. Through-out the Spanish-speaking New World, however, the animal is known as *el tigre*.

Mountain Lion

Felis concolor.   Mountain lions are widespread in New Mexico, except for the eastern plains section. They are most likely to occur in broken country, mountains, hills and badlands. Our state is one of the last places in the United States where the species seems to be holding its own. Even mountains near large urban centers, such as the Sandías, harbor a few lions.

These large cats lead solitary lives, except for the association be-tween mother and kittens, and between males and females at breeding time. Females may come into heat at any time of the year, but most are in season in spring. The males are promiscuous, staying with a given female only for the duration of her estrus. One to six young are born after a gestation of eighty-two to ninety-six days. The young are weaned by six weeks, but they remain with their mother for up to two years, when they become sexually mature. Females may continue to produce young for twelve years, but this may be toward the upper limit of the normal reproductive lifetime.

The chief prey of the mountain lion are large mammals, mostly deer in the Rocky Mountains and Southwest. It has been estimated that an adult lion can survive well on one deer per week. When deer are not plentiful, other mammals may be taken, down to and including rodents, reptiles, and birds. Occasionally, domestic livestock are killed and eaten. The incidence of such behavior probably increases when wild prey are in low numbers. The territory needed to support one lion varies with the abundance of prey, and may range from twenty-five to fifty square kilometers.

Mountain lions are also known by the common names "cougar" and "puma." Both names are of South American Indian origin, the former from Amazonia and the latter from the Andes. Names of English origin include "panther," originally from Greek and also used to refer to the leopard and the jaguar, and "catamount," which refers to other wild felids as well as the mountain lion.

Bobcat

Lynx rufus.   Bobcats are widespread and rather common in New Mexico, inhabiting rocky and broken country from the desert into forested mountains. The eastern plains section of the state seems to be less favored by the cats than the western regions.

Bobcats probably have territories, with females excluding other females and males excluding males. The territory of a male is larger than that of a female, and territories of males and females may overlap. Females come into heat in March and April. Several males may court a single female, and the female may mate with more than one male. Pregnancy lasts about ten weeks, and from one to seven kittens are produced. Males do not assist in the rearing of young. The babies are weaned at two months of age, and they may remain with the female into the fall.

Bobcats, like most other felids, hunt by stealth rather than pursuit. The cat may sit by a game trail or other strategic site until a rabbit passes nearby, and then capture the animal with a pounce or quick rush. Small and medium-sized vertebrates are the preferred prey. Lagomorphs are favored when common, and rodents, birds, and sometimes reptiles or insects are taken. Two to three square miles are required for the hunting territory of one animal.

The fur of this species has been enjoying a European vogue in recent years, and the pelts have become quite valuable. New Mexico is one among a few states that has been an important source of this item.

Even-Toed Ungulates

ORDER ARTIODACTYLA

Hooved mammals are divided into two major groups, of which artiodactyls are one. The other hooved order, the Perissodactyla, including horses, rhinos, and tapirs, is sometimes referred to as odd-toed ungulates. The common names imply that the number of toes per foot is even in one group and odd in the other. This is usually, but not always, true. Deer, bison, goats, and sheep do have an even number of toes (two or four), but the peccary has three toes on the hindfoot. Horses have one toe, but tapirs have four front toes as do some rhinos. The critical difference is not the number of toes, but the plane of symmetry of the foot. In artiodactyls the midline of the foot lies between toes three and four. Both of those toes are equally developed and bear weight equally. Toes two and five may be present, but toe number one, corresponding to the big toe or thumb on a primate, is absent. In perissodactyls the plane of symmetry runs down the middle of the third toe, which is the largest, and bears most of the weight. Toes two and three may be present, as may others. Modern horses have only the third toe on each foot. There are many other differences between these groups. Many artiodactyls have complexly divided stomachs and regurgitate their food for a second chewing. The stomach contains a rich microbial flora that helps with the chemical breakdown of food. Perissodactyls, on the other hand, uniformly lack this specialization. Those artiodactyls that practice rumination (cud-chewing) lack upper incisor teeth, and clip off vegetation by pressing it between the lower incisors and the upper gums. Perissodactyls have both upper and lower incisors, and grasp vegetation between these two tooth-rows.

New Mexican artiodactyls belong to two groups: the suborder Suina, which includes peccary and domestic swine, and the suborder Ruminantia, which contains the cud-chewing species such as deer, cattle, sheep, goats, and pronghorns. Suines lack horns or antlers in both sexes, but they possess large elongate canine teeth and both upper and lower incisors. Ruminants have either horns or antlers, at least in males, and lack upper incisors.

Two suines may be observed in the wild in New Mexico: the native peccary (*Tayassu tajacu*) and the feral domestic swine (*Sus scrofa*). The two are usually placed in different families: Tayassuidae for the native animal, and Suidae for the domestic species. Domestic pigs tend to be sparsely haired, and the upper canines of adults turn outward and upward. Peccaries are more fully haired and tend to have a collar of light-colored hairs around the top of the neck. Both species may be found living together in some of the small mountain ranges in extreme southwestern New Mexico.

Collared Peccary

Tayassu tajacu. Peccaries are restricted to the southwestern and southeastern parts of our state. The present occupied range seems to be Hidalgo, Grant, Catron, Otero, and Eddy counties. These are animals of the desert, rocky and brushy foothill regions, and riparian communities. Places where prickly pears and leguminous shrubs are common are also favored by peccaries, because of both the cover and forage provided by these plants.

Peccaries occur in bands of five to fifteen animals, including members of both sexes and all age groups. Within the band there seems to be no leadership. So far as is known, the animals are promiscuous. Mating may take place at any time of year, but the greatest number of births appear to occur in summer. Since the gestation is 142 to 149 days, the chief mating activity would seem to be in late winter or early spring. One to four, usually two, young are born. The babies are quite precocial, and are able to follow their mother in a day or two, at which time the family rejoins the group. Babies nurse for six to eight weeks, and remain with their mother for two to three months. Females attain sexual maturity at thirty-three to thirty-four weeks, and males somewhat later, at forty-six to forty-seven weeks.

The animals are chiefly herbivorous, consuming a wide variety of plant food and also a few small vertebrates. Pads of prickly pear are readily eaten, and seem to take care of some of the water needs of the javelinas. Beans of mesquite and other leguminous shrubs are also favored foods. Peccaries do spend considerable time in turning over dead vegetation, small rocks, and the like, searching for food, but apparently they do less actual rooting in the earth with their snouts than domestic pigs. In some areas of the Southwest, ranchers welcome the presence of peccaries because they are thought to exert some controlling influence over the abundance of prickly pear.

Peccaries are game animals, and the meat is quite palatable. A musk gland on the rump, probably of use to the animals in communication, must be removed by the hunter before preparing the meat for the table.

The word *peccary* is probably of Carib origin. *Javelina,* a word also commonly applied to this animal, is of Arabic origin and comes to us through Spanish; originally, it referred to the Old World wild boar.

DEER

Family Cervidae

Deer are distinguished by the presence on one or both sexes of antlers, branched structures made of bone that are used chiefly in sexual display and fighting, but which also serve as defensive weapons. Antlers are shed and regrown each year. In New Mexican species only males normally grow antlers; however, in the caribou, *Rangifer tarandrus,* of northern North America, both sexes possess them. In that species the antlers function, in part, as snow shovels to expose buried food. New Mexican male deer begin to grow their antlers in spring. By late summer the antlers are nearly full size and are covered with living tissue, termed *velvet.* When the antlers are fully developed, the velvet dies and is rubbed off. The structures are then polished and sharp-pointed. After the fall mating season, the antlers are shed. Antler growth seems to be influenced by testosterone, the male hormone produced by the testes. Castrated males lose their antlers, and does injected with testosterone are able to grow them. Antler size and the number of points is chiefly a function of the male's physical condition, and is influenced only slightly by the age of the animal.

Three species of deer are native to New Mexico: the elk, or wapiti, *Cervus elaphus;* the mule deer, *Odocoileus hemionus;* and the white-tailed deer, *O. virginianus.* The wapiti is the largest, and is distinguished by a mane of dark hair, which hangs from the bottom of the neck, and by a large oval yellowish rump patch, which extends well up onto the back. The antlers extend backward over the shoulders. *Odocoileus* deer have either white, or no, rump patches; no mane; and the antlers turn forward over the facial area. Mule deer have a whitish or grayish rump patch, and a tail that is grayish on top with a distinct black tip. Running mule deer hold the tail out straight or pointed downward. The antlers subdivide once or twice into more or less equal branches. White-tailed deer have no rump patch. The tail is dark on top, fringed with white, and is white beneath, with no black tip. Running white-tails hold their tails upward and wag them from side to side. Each antler has one main beam which curves forward and gives off smaller, upwardly directed branches. Mule deer are the deer commonly seen in most of New Mexico. White-tails are seen mostly in the mountains of the southwestern part of the state.

Mule Deer

Odocoileus hemionus. Mule deer are statewide in distribution, and, except for those areas where the white-tail is common, they occupy most habitats. Areas with little cover in the form of vegetation or of broken country are the least favored, and the animals are uncommon in the eastern plains section of the state. Where white-tailed deer are common, as in Catron, Grant, and Hidalgo counties, the white-tails occupy montane forest or riparian situations, while mule deer are more common in open and arid sections.

The basic social unit in this species is the mature doe with her fawns of one or two years. Within this group exists a dominance hierarchy, with the old doe as the alpha individual. She also leads the group in daily and seasonal movements. During the mating season, the group may be joined by one or more adult males who pursue the does as they come into estrus. Usually a dominant buck attempts to keep other bucks away from the group, but the male does not round up a harem, as male elk do. Mating occurs from October through January, depending upon latitude. Afterward, the males leave the family group, and may consort in bachelor groups or remain solitary. Gestation is 201 to 210 days. Most fawns are born in June or July in our area. One to three young are born, with two being the most common number. The spotted young are hidden by the female, and remain so for a few days; then they are able to follow the mother as she rejoins her family. Fawns lose their spots at 6 to 8 weeks of age. The young of both sexes normally do not reach sexual maturity until their second summer. Males may continue to grow for 6 to 8 years. Females are maximally fertile from 4½ to 7½ years.

Mule deer are chiefly browsers, feeding on dicotyledonous plants rather than grasses. Favored foods are the leaves and growing twigs of a variety of shrubs, referred to as "browse" by game managers. Browse is most abundant in late summer and fall, and becomes increasingly hard to find as winter progresses. Most deer lose weight during the period of low browse availability, and they gain again when times are good. Winter is a stressful time for deer populations, and many young die during this period. Seasonal movements of groups of deer result from seasonal differences in browse availability. Males are especially prone to extensive seasonal movements, but doe-led groups move as well. Late summer may see many bucks at high elevations, and winter often sees a movement to lower areas.

Early in this century deer became quite uncommon in many parts of the Southwest. In 1924 the deer herd of New Mexican national forests was estimated to be slightly in excess of 19,000 animals. By the 1960s the herd was estimated at almost 302,000. Part of this increase may be attributed to game laws and good management practices, but some of it must surely have resulted from the virtual elimination, or great reduction, of the deer's natural large predators, the mountain lion and the wolf. In effect, man has had to compensate for that loss by carefully controlling the herds through regulated hunting. Overpopulated deer habitat quickly suffers from the overbrowsing, and the ability of such a place to support deer is greatly reduced.

White-Tailed Deer

Odocoileus virginianus.   White-tailed deer are rather common in the southwestern part of the state, but are rarely found in other areas. Almost all of our known records are from mountainous regions. While little is known of the habits of this species in our area, the species has been well studied in other places. Most of the generalizations made concerning feeding, social life, and reproduction for the mule deer also apply to this species.

Elk

Cervus elaphus.   In the early days elk, or wapiti, were found in most of the montane regions of New Mexico. Those occupying the southwestern mountain ranges were considered a separate species: the Merriam elk, *C. merriami*. The Merriam elk, as well as all other elk populations in the state, were essentially exterminated by 1909. Efforts to reintroduce the elk from other areas began almost immediately. By 1912 there were about 60 elk in the state; by 1923, 750; by 1934, perhaps 4,000; and by 1967, almost 11,000. The formerly occupied range was once again utilized by the species. The Merriam elk was, in all likelihood, a local race of the wide-ranging *C. elaphus*.

The elk social unit is a herd of cows and calves numbering from forty to well over a hundred individuals. These are more than simply the family groups seen in *Odocoileus*. Bull elk become ready for mating in September and October, when their antlers are fully developed and they grow extremely aggressive. The males attempt to acquire harems of as many cows as possible, and they try to defend these females from being mated by other males. The size of the harem, from fifteen to thirty, depends upon the age and size of the bull. Younger males are less successful than older ones, and the youngest must be content with sneaking an occasional mating when the master of the harem is occupied elsewhere. During this season the males may fight, and they announce their presence by loud vocalizations that have been referred to as bugling. After October or November, the males drop their antlers and leave the company of the cows, who go back to their herd relationships with other cows and with youngsters.

Gestation is about 8½ months. The female leaves the herd to have her one or two calves, but she returns within a few days when the youngsters are old enough to follow. Like other deer, baby elk are spotted, but the spots are lost by the end of the summer. Male elk are sexually mature at two years of age, but are probably rather unsuccessful at siring offspring until they are older. Females are capable of breeding at two years, but may wait until they are almost four.

Unlike *Odocoileus*, the elk is a grazer, a feeder upon grass. Elk graze in mountain meadows, and when these are covered too deeply by snow they migrate to lower elevations. In the early days, through much of the Rocky Mountain region, elk moved out into the plains in winter, where they often competed with cattle for grass. With the fencing of the West such migrations became impossible, and this has made life more difficult for elk, except in those places where man has provided winter forage for them. Fences, along with human hunters, are the chief modern dangers for elk.

The common name of this animal in North America is elk. But in the western part of Eurasia the term *elk* (spelled *elch* in northern Europe) applies to the animal that Americans call moose, *Alces alces*. The species *Cervus elaphus* is found across northern Eurasia, however, and receives a number of other common names there. In Britain, where the animal has been intensively studied, it is known as the red deer. The males are known as stags and the females as hinds. Here, we use the terms *bull* and *cow*. Because of this nomenclatural confusion, there has long been a move in North America to use the Shawnee word *wapiti*. This has never caught on except in books, and it is not clear why we should adopt the word used by one of the many native American groups who named *Cervus elaphus* before the arrival of Europeans. Almost all Americans use the word *elk*. However, *Cervus* comes from the Latin *cerva*, meaning deer. The English word *deer* applied originally to *C. elaphus* (and latterly to other members of the deer family), and has a long and respectable history of usage for this animal. In the interests of uniformity, it would seem reasonable to refer to North American populations of *C. elaphus* as red deer.

SHEEP, GOATS, CATTLE

Family: Bovidae

Animals belonging to this family are called horned ruminants because they possess true horns consisting of a bone core and an external sheath, and because they have a multichambered stomach which enables them to regurgitate food for additional chewing, a behavior known as rumination or cud-chewing. Bovids are the most specialized large grazing mammals. Most have very elongate distal segments to their legs, which are specialized for rapid locomotion, and most are inhabitants of open grasslands.

Rumination is an adaptation that helps an herbivorous grassland mammal in at least two ways. Since stems and foliage, especially those of grasses, are difficult to process mechanically as well as chemically, the possession of a complex stomach harboring microorganisms that have the ability to break down cellulose, the tough material of plant cell walls, makes possible a degree of chemical digestion of this common food not available to many other animals. The ability to rapidly ingest large quantities of low-quality food, store it in a specialized stomach chamber, and then regurgitate it later for leisurely chewing allows the animals to minimize the time spent in food gathering, when they are most vulnerable to predation. Later, in the relative safety of a shelter, the mechanical processing of the vegetation can take place.

Bovids are the common large grazing mammals of Eurasia and Africa, but relatively few have ever entered the New World. Those species that have arrived in North America have come across the Bering straits, and only cold-adapted species have been able to make the trek. The exception is the pronghorn, *Antilocapra,* whose ancestors arrived at an early date and became specialized for the relatively temperate grasslands of the central and southern part of the continent.

New Mexican bovids include the pronghorn, *Antilocapra americana;* the mountain sheep, *Ovis canadensis;* and the bison, *Bison bison.* In addition, several non-native bovids have been introduced. These include the Barbary sheep, *Ammotragus lervia;* the domestic goat, *Capra hircus;* the ibex, *Capra ibex;* and the oryx, *Oryx gazella.* Of these, only the Barbary sheep is at all widespread. The horns of the pronghorn are distinctive in shape: the tips bend toward the rear of the animal, and there is a forward-pointing short prong. Mountain sheep have horns that curve backward, sometimes making a complete coil, and which possess raised ridges running around them like rings. Barbary sheep might be confused with mountain sheep, but male Barbarys have a mane of long hair hanging from the ventral midline of the neck. Mountain sheep lack this mane. Bison have short horns that curve upward and forward, are the size of cows, have high shoulders, and are dark brown. Ibex and goats might be confused with mountain sheep or Barbarys, but the males have beards rather than manes, like a male Barbary. Oryx have very long, nearly straight horns, and might be seen only in the White Sands area.

Pronghorn

Antilocapra americana. The horns of *Antilocapra* are distinctive in that their sheaths are shed once a year and regrown. Pronghorns are not likely to be confused with any other large grazing mammal. The two white throat patches, the large white rump patch, and the distinctive horns make the animals readily identifiable.

Pronghorns are widespread in the grasslands of New Mexico. Like other large mammals, they were once hunted so intensively that the entire western United States held only twelve thousand animals by about 1900. Wise management reversed this decline, however. By 1967 the number in New Mexico alone was estimated at fifteen thousand, and the state herd was estimated at thirty thousand in 1984.

During the spring and summer, male pronghorns consort in bachelor herds. Females and their young forage in separate herds. In fall the males establish territories, which they defend against other males. As the herds of female and young pronghorns forage through and in the vicinity of the male territories, the resident males associate with the females and mating takes place. After the season is over, the males leave their territories and drop their horn sheaths. Gestation lasts from 230 to 250 days. The young, usually two, are born in mid-June. The young really are "dropped," with the females giving birth while in a standing position. The babies are quickly able to follow their mother, and the new family then rejoins the herd.

Pronghorns are chiefly browsers, with grass comprising less than 1 percent of the diet. Various shrubs and forbs provide the mainstay. Sage is often one of the foods most commonly taken.

Mountain Sheep

Ovis canadensis.   Bighorns live in rugged mountainous areas of cliffs and rocks adjacent to suitable feeding areas, which are places with grass and browse plants. Originally, the animals inhabited most New Mexican mountains and badlands, but intensive hunting eliminated them from most of those places by 1927, when they were reported living only in the Hatchet, San Andreas, and Guadalupe mountains. Since that time, mountain sheep have been reintroduced into the Pecos, Sandía, and Peloncillo mountains, and into the Gila, San Francisco, and Cimarron drainages. The sheep are nowhere common, and competition from the introduced Barbary sheep may make it difficult for the native species to persist where the two coexist.

Bighorns are highly social animals, as are most sheep. During most of the year, adult males occur in all male groups, and the females and younger animals similarly consort. Male groups and female groups each have home ranges, but these are not defended and may overlap broadly. Before the fall mating season begins, the males engage in fights and displays to establish a dominance hierarchy. Fighting typically involves a display jump followed by a charge, culminating in a head-to-head collision. The horns and frontal region of the skull are especially designed to help the males withstand these jarring contests. Generally, the males with the largest horns end up high in the pecking order. When the females come into heat, the males enter the female herd to seek out receptive individuals. Once a male locates a suitable mate, he attempts to defend her against other males, with varying degrees of success. After the mating season, males gradually leave the group of females and their young, to form their bachelor herds.

Gestation is about 175 days. A few days before giving birth, the female leaves the group and seeks a rugged area which affords her some protection from predators. Usually a single baby is born, although twinning occurs infrequently. The females have only two nipples. Lambs quickly begin following the mother, and some consumption of solid food may begin at two weeks of age. Weaning is completed by four to six months of age. Males grow faster than females and continue to grow longer, up to eight years, as opposed to three or four years for females. Females mate first at about thirty months of age, while males first succeed in mating much later, usually at seven to eight years old.

Sheep are primarily grazers, but a variety of browse plants are consumed as well. Minerals required in the diet may be obtained from natural salt licks. Populations living in montane areas may be able to gain enough moisture from their food, but desert animals need access to surface water.

Bison

Bison bison.   Bison are predominantly grazing animals of open grassland. In some parts of the former range of the species in North America, they were found in forest-edge and prairie–forest transition areas. In New Mexico most bison were found in the plains east of the Sangre de Cristo–Sandía–Manzano–Capitán–Sacramento mountain axis. The animals did not occur in the Rio Grande Valley or in the lands to the west. Pueblo Indians made hunting trips east of the mountains to capture the bison they needed. Bison were essentially gone from New Mexico by 1860, with the last kill recorded in 1884. Taos Indians hunted bison in the eastern plains until 1883. At the present time there are no wild bison in the state, although several captive herds exist.

Bison occur in large groups throughout the year. Females and young, including males up to three years of age, form groups of ten to twenty animals. Older males are solitary or occur in all-male groups. During the mating season, in middle to late summer, the bulls begin to mix with the cows, and may mate sequentially with a number of females. Gestation is 9½ months, with most births taking place in spring. One or two young are born, and the youngsters begin to follow the mother within a few hours after birth. Young animals of both sexes reach sexual maturity at about three years of age, but males do little breeding until they are about eight years old.

Primarily grazers, bison seem capable of growing and maintaining good condition on less nutritious fare than domestic cattle require. Bison are sometimes raised for human consumption, and are sometimes crossed with cattle ("beefalo"). A chief obstacle to more widespread commercial use is the personality of the species, which makes them somewhat more difficult to herd and manage than domestic cattle. Perhaps, however, more pounds of bison can be raised, acre for acre, on poor rangeland.

Bison also occur in eastern Europe, where a controlled herd is maintained in eastern Poland. A Germanic name for the animal in Europe is *wisent*, which is a direct cognate of the English word *bison*. The word *buffalo*, which is often applied to the bison in North America, is derived from the Greek word *boubalos*, referring to an African gazelle.

Exotic Mammals

At least eight kinds of mammals, which were not present in New Mexico at the time of the first Spanish occupancy, have been intentionally introduced or have escaped from domestication to establish feral populations. Three other species—the house mouse, the Norway rat, and the black rat—were introduced unintentionally (and have been described in the preceding pages).

Two of the introduced species that remain to be discussed are perissodactyls; four are artiodactyls; and one is a rodent.

The rodent is the nutria, *Myocaster coypus*, described on page 113. Nutrias occur at San Simon Cienega in Hidalgo County, along the Pecos near Roswell and Bitter Lakes Refuge, and along the Rio Hondo in Lincoln County.

Two of the exotic mammals are goats. The ibex, *Capra ibex*, which is native to Europe, northern Africa, the Near East, and Central Asia, was introduced into the Canadian River gorge in 1975. A wild stock of the domestic goat, *Capra hircus*, was introduced into the Florida Mountains in 1970. These animals have been quite successful, as introduced goats have been generally, and now they also occur in the Little Floridas, the Tres Hermanas, West Potrillo, Alamo Hueco, Doña Ana, and Mimbres mountains.

The Barbary sheep, *Ammotragus lervia*, was introduced into the Hondo Valley in the 1940s, and into the Canadian River gorge in the 1950s. Now the animals occur over the east side and across the northern part of the state. Barbarys are natives of northern Africa.

The oryx, *Oryx gazella,* a native of sub-Saharan Africa, was introduced in the White Sands area between 1969 and 1977. These spectacular animals have spread slightly and seem to be doing well.

Horses (*Equus caballus*) and burros (*E. asinus*) both occur throughout the Southwest as feral animals, although they are now much less common than formerly. New Mexican wild horses are confined to Rio Arriba and Socorro counties, and the only wild burros survive currently in Lincoln County.

Wild domestic swine, *Sus scrofa,* occur in a few canyons in Hidalgo and Lincoln counties.

Glossary

AUDITORY BULLA.   One of a pair of globular rounded or ovoid hollow bony structures located on the posteroventral surface of the skull surrounding the middle ear.

ANGULAR PROCESS.   A projection of bone extending posteroventrally from the posteroventral edge of the dentary, or jawbone.

ANTLER.   One of a pair of branched bony structures growing from the forehead of members of the deer family. Antlers are shed and regrown annually. With the exception of caribou and reindeer, they are found only on males.

ANTORBITAL FENESTRA.   An opening on the side of the rostrum, just in front of the zygomatic arch (not to be confused with the *infraorbital foramen,* which see).

BASILAR LENGTH.   See SKULL LENGTH.

BONY PALATE.   A plate of bone extending across the roof of the mouth between the tooth-rows.

BROW TINE.   The first anterior branch of an antler extending far forward over the forehead in elk and caribou.

BULLAR LENGTH.   See AUDITORY BULLA.

BUNODONT.   A term describing tooth cusps that are low and rounded.

CALCAR.   A cartilaginous rod extending from the ankle of some bats medially toward the tail and supporting the trailing edge of the uropatagium.

CANINE.   A large pointed tooth behind the incisor teeth in each tooth-row. In the upper row it is the first tooth in the maxillary bone. There are a maximum of four.

CHEEK TOOTH.   A term usually referring to molars and premolars.

CINGULUM.   A shelf around the base of a tooth just above the gum line.

CONDYLOBASAL LENGTH.   See SKULL LENGTH.

CORONOID PROCESS.   A vertical plate of bone on the posterodorsal surface of the dentary bone, or jawbone, forming the insertion area for the temporal muscle.

CUSP.   A projection on the chewing (occlusal) surface of a tooth. Cusps may be pointed, rounded, or have other more complicated shapes.

DENTARY RAMUS.   The dentary is the lower jawbone. The horizontal part of the bone bearing the teeth is the dentary ramus.

DENTINE.   A bonelike material which forms the inner part of teeth.

DIASTEMA.   A toothless space or gap in a tooth-row.

EAR LENGTH.   The distance from the tip of the ear pinna to the bottom (proximalmost border) of the notch behind the tragus.

EMARGINATE.   A term referring to the shape of an object that is cut in such a way that its edge shows one or more sharp indentations.

ENAMEL.   An extremely hard, often shiny material covering the exposed surface of a tooth, largely composed of calcium phosphate.

FORAMEN MAGNUM.   The large hole on the back of the skull through which the spinal cord passes to join the brain.

GREATEST SKULL LENGTH.   See SKULL LENGTH.

HINDFOOT LENGTH.   The distance from the posteriormost surface of the heel to the front of the nail or claw on the longest toe.

HORN.   One of a pair of bony projections from the forehead of members of the cattle family, covered with a sheath of material derived from the skin. Horn sheaths of pronghorns are shed annually, but those of other bovids are not.

INCISIVE FORAMEN.   See PALATINE FORAMEN.

INCISOR.   The first teeth in each tooth-row are ordinarily incisors. In the upper tooth-row, they are inserted in the premaxillary bone. There are a maximum of six above and six below.

INFRAORBITAL CANAL (FORAMEN).   An opening extending from the eye socket or orbital fossa anteriorly through the anterior root of the zygomatic arch to the side of the rostrum in rodents. If it is a simple hole through a plate of bone, it is called a foramen; if it is tubular, it is called a canal.

INTERFEMORAL MEMBRANE.   See UROPATAGIUM.

INTERORBITAL BREADTH.   A skull dimension measured across the top of the skull between the medialmost points of the eye sockets or orbital fossae.

INTERPARIETAL.   An unpaired skull bone located on the roof of the braincase just dorsal to its posterior surface.

INTERPTERYGOID FOSSA.   A depression or trough on the ventral surface of the skull receiving the internal narial openings and bordered laterally by thin walls of bone bearing posteriorly directed points, the pterygoid processes.

KEEL.   A cartilaginous flap on the posterior edge of the calcar of bats.

LABIAL.   Referring to the lips. The labial side of a tooth is the side toward the lips.

LINGUAL.   Referring to the tongue. The lingual side of the tooth is the side toward the tongue.

MANDIBLE.   The lower jaw, composed of the two dentary bones.

MASTOID BREADTH.   A skull measurement of width taken across the back of the skull between the lateralmost extensions of the mastoid bones, which are exposed just behind the ear opening.

MAXILLARY BREADTH.   A width measurement of the skull, usually equivalent to *rostral breadth* (see ROSTRAL BREADTH), but referring specifically to that part of the rostrum made up of the maxillary bones.

MAXILLARY TOOTH-ROW.   Comprised of those upper teeth situated in the maxillary bone. Canines, premolars, and molars are maxillary teeth.

MENTAL FORAMEN.   One of a pair of small holes located on the anterolateral surface of the dentary bone, or jawbone.

MOLAR.   One of the posterior teeth in a tooth-row, often flattened and useful for grinding or crushing. There are a maximum of three in each tooth-row. Molars are not preceded by milkteeth; hence, molar teeth are not replaced.

NASAL.   One of a pair of elongate skull bones forming the dorsal surface of the rostrum.

NASAL SEPTUM.   On peering into the palatine foramen (see PALANTINE FORAMEN), one may see a thin vertical sheet of bone separating the two halves of the nasal chamber, the *nasal septum.*

NOSE LEAF.   A pointed fold of skin extending vertically above the nose of bats of the family Phyllostomatidae.

OCCIPITAL CONDYLE.   One of a pair of rounded processes, located on either side of the foramen magnum, which articulate with sockets in the first vertebra.

OCCIPITONASAL LENGTH.   See SKULL LENGTH.

OCCLUSAL.   Referring to the chewing surface of a tooth.

PALATINE FORAMEN.   One of two pairs of anteroposteriorly elongate openings in the bony palate. In most rodents a single pair is present, often referred to as *incisive foramina.*

PARIETAL-SQUAMOSAL SUTURE. The dividing line between the parietal bone (located on the side of the braincase) and the squamosal bone (which bears the posterior root of the zygomatic arch).

PARIETAL. One of a pair of skull bones which make up the sides of the braincase.

PENTADACTYL. Having five toes.

PHALANX. The bone of a single segment of a finger or toe.

PINNA. The external ear flap.

PLAGIOPATAGIUM. The part of the flight membrane of a bat extending from the side of the body and bordered by the arm, the fifth finger, and the hind leg.

POSTERIOR NARIAL CAVITY. The opening into the nasal chamber above and behind the bony palate (see BONY PALATE).

POSTORBITAL PROCESS. One of a pair of slender projections of bone extending in a posterolateral direction from the top of the skull over the posterior border of the eye socket or orbital fossa.

PREMAXILLA. One of a pair of skull bones making up the sides of the anterior part of the rostrum and bearing incisor teeth.

PREMOLAR. A tooth located behind the canine and in front of the molars.

PROCUMBENT. A term describing front teeth, usually incisors, which protrude forward from the tooth-row.

REËNTRANT ANGLE. On the occlusal surface of certain cheek teeth, such as those of voles and wood rats, the cusps may be partially separated from one another by V-shaped indentations, the *reëntrant angles.*

ROSTRAL BREADTH. A skull measurement taken across the widest part of the rostrum.

ROSTRUM. The snout region of the skull in front of the eye sockets.

SAGITTAL CREST. A ridge of bone running along the dorsal midline of the braincase of some mammals.

SKULL LENGTH. A measurement of the anteroposterior length of a skull. Because the skulls of different kinds of mammals are differently shaped, it is not always convenient to measure length in the same way on every skull. Thus, different sorts of skull lengths are used for different groups of mammals, as follows:

Basilar length. From the anteromost point of the ventral border of the foramen magnum to the posterior border of the sockets of the first incisors.

Condylobasal length. From the posteromost margin of the occipital condyles to the anteromost margin of the premaxillary bones.

Greatest skull length.   The greatest possible anteroposterior dimension of the skull, excluding teeth.

Occipitonasal length.   From the posteromost extension of the braincase to the anteromost projection of the nasal bones.

SUPRAOCCIPITAL SHIELD.   A flattened surface of bone on the midline of the posterodorsal part of the braincase of rabbits and hares.

SUPRAORBITAL PROCESS.   A shelf of bone extending from the top of the skull over the eye socket or orbital fossa in rabbits and hares.

TEMPORAL RIDGE.   A raised border of bone running across the dorsolateral part of the braincase, marking the dorsal border of the temporal muscle. If the temporal muscles extend to the dorsal midline of the braincase, the temporal ridges fuse, forming the sagittal crest.

TERETE.   Referring to the condition of the tip of a tail that is not clothed in long hairs.

TOTAL LENGTH (of mammal).   The distance between the tip of the nose and the tip of the skin, not hair, of the tail when the animal is laid on its back and stretched to its fullest extent, without separating the vertebrae.

TRAGUS.   A rounded or elongate flap partly obstructing the external ear opening.

TRUNCATE.   A term referring to the shape of an object that is cut off squarely, as opposed to pointed or indented.

UNICUSPID.   A term referring to certain single-cusped teeth of shrews that lie between the large procumbent first teeth and the multicuspid cheek teeth. Because the identity of these teeth is not certain, they are referred to by this descriptive term.

UROPATAGIUM.   That part of the flight membrane of a bat extending between the hind leg and the tail.

VOMER.   A vertical plate of bone partially dividing the nasal chamber. In deer, the vomer may be seen by looking into the internal narial opening of the skull above and behind the palate.

ZYGOMATIC ARCH.   A narrow bridge of bone below the eye socket extending from front to back. The cheek bone.

Further Reading

All of the states bordering on New Mexico have been the subject of mammalian studies. Titles of other books on New Mexican mammals, as well as references to the books on adjacent states, follow.

Anderson, S. 1972. *Mammals of Chihuahua.* American Museum of Natural History Bulletin 148:151–410. New York.

Armstrong, D. 1972. *Distribution of mammals in Colorado,* Museum of Natural History Monographs, University of Kansas, 3:1–415. Lawrence.

Bailey, V. 1932. *Mammals of New Mexico.* North American Fauna 53:1–412. Washington. (The date appearing on the volume is 1931. The true date of publication, however, was 1932.)

Caire, W. 1978. *Mammals of Sonora.* Ph.D. diss. University of New Mexico, Alburquerque. 613 pp.

Cockrum, E. L. 1960. *The Recent mammals of Arizona.* University of Arizona Press, Tucson. 276 pp.

Davis, W. B. 1966. *The mammals of Texas.* Texas Parks and Wildlife Department Bulletin 41:1–267. Austin.

Durrant, S. D. 1952. *Mammals of Utah.* University of Kansas Publications, Museum of Natural History, 6:1–549. Lawrence.

Findley, J. S., A. H. Harris, D. E. Wilson, and C. Jones. 1975. *Mammals of New Mexico.* University of New Mexico Press, Albuquerque. 360 pp.

Two very useful general references on mammals are:

Vaughan, T. A. 1978. *Mammalogy.* Saunders College Publishing, Philadelphia. 522 pp.

Walker, E. P. 1975. *Mammals of the World.* Johns Hopkins University Press, Baltimore. Two volumes.

The American Society of Mammalogists is the chief organization for professional mammalogists in the New World. The Society was founded in 1919, and in that year began publication of the *Journal of Mammalogy*, which has appeared four times a year since that date. The Journal is the world's leading source of original research articles dealing with all aspects of the biology of mammals. The Society also publishes *Mammalian Species*, a series of pamphlets each of which summarizes the known information about a species of mammal. The series began in 1969, and 263 accounts had been issued by the end of 1985.

All of the references cited here may be consulted in the libraries of New Mexico's state universities. Further information about the American Society of Mammalogists or its publications may be obtained by writing the secretary-treasurer.

INDEX

159

Date Due